# The Growth of Shipbuilding

The engineering skills to construct and complete the Grand Canal were very advanced, enabling certain sections to be built over mountains. Locks, sluice gates and reservoirs were employed to control the water level. The canal also spurred shipbuilding, giving shipwrights the opportunity to design ships not only specifically for individual types of goods, but also to ply certain sections of the canal – the wide or narrow, deep or shallow. Chinese seafarers were also the first to use rudders as well as watertight compartments, transverse bulkheads, single masts and square sails.

Giant bamboo and wood were important materials in the construction of Chinese vessels. Being light and extremely strong, bamboo made strong masts. It went into booms and yards of the lugsails, and was attached to the sails at regular intervals for added strength and protection. Bamboo supports made sails easier to unfurl, particularly during storms.

Chinese shipbuilders pioneered the use of aft and fore rigging: sails were not aligned at right angles to the ship but rather along the ship's length, enabling the ship to sail very close to the wind and even into the wind. This innovation of the 3rd century A.D. would appear in European ship design with the arrival of the Portuguese in the 15th century, more than a thousand years later.

**A** Spanish galleon approaches shore in this 19th century depiction opposite, top. Opposite, below: Artist's impression of a treasure ship, complete with dragon eye on the bow of the ship.

With another Chinese invention, the paddle wheel, men sailed ships by operating a treadle. Paddle-wheel ships were effective in military manoeuvres, according to one account of a naval battle in A.D. 418. The Song dynasty (A.D. 960–1271) saw the development of fast-moving rudderless paddle-wheel warships.

Oceangoing junks like the treasure ships were steered by a rudder attached to the stern and bottom of the ship. Rudders appear in 5th and 6th century Chinese shipbuilding texts, but clay models of ships with central axial rudders have been unearthed in Han tombs dating many centuries earlier. Western shipbuilding only incorporated central axial rudders some 1,100 years after Han times.

Some say the shape of the oceangoing junk – resembling a halved hollow cylinder – was inspired by the shape of a short section of bamboo with curving ends. The base of the ship was flat and its bow and stern square-ended, without stem posts or stern posts. The transverse bulkheads greatly strengthened the whole hull and also acted as watertight compartments, while other compartments at the bow and stern could be freely flooded to gain or lose ballast.

With science and the stars in their grasp, no wonder the Ming period saw the flowering of shipbuilding and navigation skills in the form of the treasure fleet. The ships were the largest wooden ships the world had ever seen. And it would take all of China's scientific knowhow to ensure they were furnished to fulfil Zheng He's mission to the satisfaction of his emperor.

# Zheng He and China's Islamic Tradition

The expeditions of the treasure fleet were entrusted to Admiral Zheng He and a select group of high-ranking eunuchs. Zheng He the man is a bit of an enigma. He left no writings of his own that have survived to our time and there is no contemporary biography about him. What we know about the man comes from secondary sources and that too mainly written after the end of the voyages.

## The Admiral's Background

Zheng He adopted a nephew, who carried on his name and whose descendants today trace their lineage back to Zheng He. From the oral traditions of Zheng He's descendants we learn of the admiral's capture as a young boy in Yunnan province. The story goes that the young Zheng He, then called Ma He, impressed his captors so much with his intelligence that he was put into the service of Zhudi, the fourth son of the emperor and the future Yongle emperor of China. Zheng He proved himself an adept military commander and assisted Zhudi in all of his military campaigns, including the rebellion that was to catapult Zhudi to the Dragon Throne.

Physical descriptions of Zheng He left to us highlight just how special he was. A mid-15th century text *Gu jin shi jian (Things past or present known or seen)* describes the admiral as seven feet tall with a waist about five feet in girth. High cheekbones and forehead and

a small nose framed "glaring eyes", while his teeth were "white and well-shaped as shells". His voice was "as loud as a huge bell".[1]

We also know a little about Islam in China during the Yuan and Ming periods. It was the religion Zheng He adhered to all his life and possibly one of the many reasons he was chosen to command the voyages, which were mainly to places that had a strong Islamic influence. Indeed, ongoing studies are investigating whether the treasure fleet helped the spread of Islam in Southeast Asia, given that the fleet probably carried many Chinese Muslims who may have settled down at various ports in the Indonesian archipelago instead of returning to China.

## Islam in China[2]

Islam has had a long history in China, and its first adherents appeared in the country quite soon after the religion was founded by Prophet Mohammed in 7th century Arabia. It entered by two routes – the overland Silk Road into China's northwestern regions and the maritime Spice Route to China's southern coastal regions.

The Chinese Muslims today are generally regarded to be descendants of central Asians, Persians and Arabs who moved to China for various reasons – trade or through conquest by the Mongol empire in the 13th century. Arab and Persian merchants who came to China via the sea route settled around ports like Quanzhou, Changzhou and Guangzhou in the south. To speak of a single Muslim community in China, therefore, is inaccurate. They are spread out throughout China, speak different languages and belong to different socio-economic groups.

## A Diverse Community

Ten Muslim ethnic groups have been accorded official minority status by the state. These are the Uighurs, Kazakhs, Kyrgyz, Uzbeks, Tatars, Tajiks, Salars, Bao'an, Dongxiang and Hui. They speak dialects belonging to the Tibetan, Turkic, Mongolian and Chinese languages. Geographically, Islamic communities are most visible in northwestern China, along the famed Silk Road, in the provinces of Gansu, Qinghai and Shaanxi, as well as the autonomous regions of Ningxia and Xinjiang.

A Hui Muslim man in Xi'an sports the white cap that identifies him as a member of that community.

Unlike Turkic-speaking Muslim groups found mainly in the northwest, the Muslim Hui peoples are found all over China, including the south, where they are the major Muslim minority. What further distinguishes the Hui from other Muslim groups in China is their use of Chinese as a lingua franca and the degree to which they appear to be more sinicised than the other groups. Most of them look no different from Han Chinese.

Interestingly enough, there are also differences between the various Hui communities, with the Hui in the northwestern regions displaying more Islamic character than their counterparts in the southern coastal regions.

Young Muslims in a mosque in Yunnan province.

# Ming Period Muslims

Zheng He's Muslim family lived in China's mountainous southwest region, in Kunyang, south of Kunming, the capital of Yunnan province. Zheng He's original name was Ma He, Ma being a common Chinese derivative of Mohammed. His grandfather and father both carried the title Haji, which indicates that they had made the *haj*, or pilgrimage to Mecca.[3]

His family is believed to be descended from Muslims who settled in Yunnan during the Mongol conquest of China and the early years of the Mongol Yuan dynasty. The Mongol expansion into Central Asia and eventual control of China saw a vast displacement of people, some fleeing the Mongol armies, or later, as new arrivals to China.

Some records[4] say that Zheng He's forefathers may have come to Kunming together with Sayid Ajall, a Turkic ruler of Buhkara in present-day Uzbekistan, during Kublai Khan's conquest of Yunnan. Ajall became the governor of Kunming in 1274 and established a strong Central Asian Muslim presence in Yunnan that can still be seen today.

The early Ming period saw considerable ethnic and religious diversity in China. The incoming Ming dynasty continued to rely on Mongol and Muslim citizens in many walks of life, including in military and naval service. Muslims did, however, suffer discrimination, possibly because of their role as tax collectors during the preceding Mongol Yuan dynasty.

**This Chinese mosque in a Yunnan province village resembles a typical Daoist temple.**

The Ashab mosque in Quanzhou, with its beautiful 11th century minaret, bears a number of inscriptions from no less than the Yongle emperor himself. The emperor declares that all mosques are to be protected, that Muslims are "good", "sincere" subjects who are loyal and "most deserving of commendation", that "official, military and civilian [households] and other categories of people shall not maltreat, insult, cheat or bully" Muslims, and that whoever flaunts this prohibition "shall be punished according to the crime".[5] That the emperor had to issue this personal edict indicates that Muslims faced prejudice during his reign, but it is clear that discrimination was not tolerated at the official level judging by the Ashab mosque inscriptions.

**B**eautiful Yunnan alpine scenery, complete with snowclad mountains and green meadows.

# Zheng He's China Today

## Yunnan[6]

Situated in southwest China and bordering Myanmar, Laos and Vietnam, Yunnan is one of China's most diverse provinces in terms of both natural and human landscape. Within its borders are found half of China's floral and faunal species and 25 different ethnic groups. The western and northern reaches of Yunnan feature ice-capped mountains, plunging ravines and raging rivers, while the southern areas are moist and tropical. Zheng He was born in Yunnan province and the Muslim Hui people are just one of the province's many ethnic communities.

**T**he mosque in Wenming village, Yunnan province, with domes and arched windows.

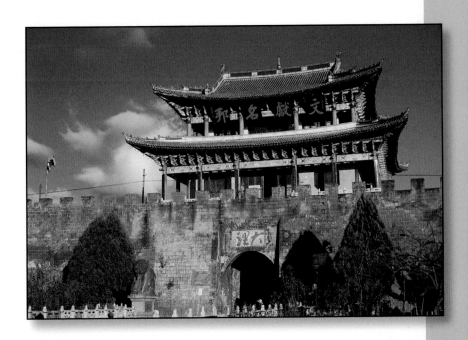

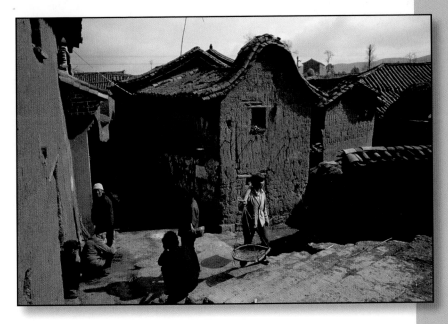

**S**cenes of Yunnan: (opposite) a peninsula in Lake Lugu; (top) the old city gate in Dali in the northern part of Yunnan; (below) village life in rural Yunnan.

# Kunming

Yunnan's capital, Kunming, offers visitors the fascinating Yunnan Provincial Museum. The large museum building resembles a Soviet-style municipal edifice, but the interior dazzles with displays of Yunnan's cultural treasures. Precious jewellery from the various ethnic groups rests beside musical instruments and rich costumes and textiles. The enormous jewellery collection ranges from earrings to bangles, from belts to necklaces, and from armbands to rings.

The museum also displays Yunnan's ancient bronzes that date from the 4th century B.C. Whether drums, mirrors, sewing boxes, weapons, farm implements or figurines, these bronzes testify to ancient Yunnan's rich and sophisticated civilisation. The bronzes take pride of place among the museum's possessions and feature vivid depictions of early life in Yunnan, including domestic scenes, royal audiences, and farming and religious ceremonies.

Close to the Yunnan Provincial Museum is Kunming's Muslim quarter. Here Chinese Muslim restaurants serve lamb and beef dishes. Mosques in Kunming, like those in Xi'an and Beijing – two other cities with a significant number of Chinese Muslims – display both Arabic and Chinese architectural styles.

**M**inority Yi lady decked out in the colourful costume of her ethnic group.

# Zheng He Park and Museum

On the southern shores of Lake Dianchi, south of Kunming, visitors can learn about Zheng He and the voyages of the treasure fleet at the Zheng He Gongyuan, a park and museum complex set in sprawling grounds. The museum takes the form of a beautiful Buddhist temple. Inside are rubbings from many different steles that describe Zheng He's travels, including one from a stele now called the Zheng He inscription stone. The original stele, erected in Quanzhou in Fujian province, still stands in that coastal city.

**A** peaceful lake in Daguan Park in Kunming, the capital of Yunnan (below) and a tiny hamlet in the Yunnan countryside surrounded by green rice terraces (opposite).

Other exhibits include cargo of the treasure ships and photographs of various places at which they docked. Contemporary paintings attempt to reconstruct some of the stories of Zheng He's meetings with foreigners. The museum displays a scaled-down model of a treasure ship, with charts and lists detailing the staggering dimensions of of the original. Wall-mounted maps indicate the routes of the seven historic voyages, and the various ports that the treasure fleet visited.

In the park is the tomb of Zheng He's father, its original stele carved 600 years ago. The stele narrates Zheng He's family history and portrays Zheng He's father as "diligent, clear-headed and sharp-witted; modest, respectful, strict and close-mouthed".[7]

## Quanzhou

Quanzhou on the coast of Fujian province was a major port throughout the Song and Yuan and early Ming periods. A sizeable Arab and Persian community established itself in Quanzhou, for the maritime Spice Route in Southeast Asia terminated in the city.

The Arabs called Quanzhou Zaiton. It was visited by the famous Arab traveller Ibn-Battuta during his Asian voyages between 1325 and 1355.

Marco Polo described the city as "a great resort of ships and merchandise from India" and the greatest port in the world after Alexandria in Egypt. In 1974, a Song dynasty (A.D. 960–1271) ocean junk was discovered in the silted bay of the port. Its cargo remains of

spices and exotic woods provide testimony to Quanzhou's illustrious past as a major Chinese coastal city that grew rich on the spice trade.

Today, the once thriving port is a quiet place, having surrendered its status as a result of the silting of the harbour and the growth of other ports to the north and south. Its ancient Muslim character is also not very evident. However, one of Quanzhou's mosques, the Qingzhen mosque, harks back to China's maritime past. The mosque is one of the oldest in the country, dating to 1010. It was rebuilt in 1310. One of its gates is said to be a replica of a gate in Damascus, Syria, at the other end of the Silk Road.

Quanzhou's cemetery, the Cemetery of the Sacred Tombs of the Sages, also bears witness to China's multi-religious past, with its stone memorials carved with Arabic and Chinese words.

It is from Quanzhou that Zheng He embarked on the fifth voyage of the treasure fleet, to far-off Hormuz. Interviews conducted by Louise Levathes for her book *When China Ruled the Seas* indicate that Zheng He is alive in the minds of some of Quanzhou's residents. Boatmen of Baiqi, a small Muslim village just north of Quanzhou, told her stories handed down by their forefathers. Zheng He had played Chinese chess with the villagers when he visited the place in 1417 to recruit seamen for the fifth voyage of the treasure fleet. The villagers spoke of the ingenuity and strength of Baiqi sailors who helped extricate a treasure ship that had run aground off Java during the fifth voyage.

Arabic and Chinese characters greet visitors as they pass under the entrance gateway of the Jinbilu mosque (left) in Kunming, Yunnan province. Right: Arabic calligraphy and Islamic motifs adorn this Chinese ceramic vase .

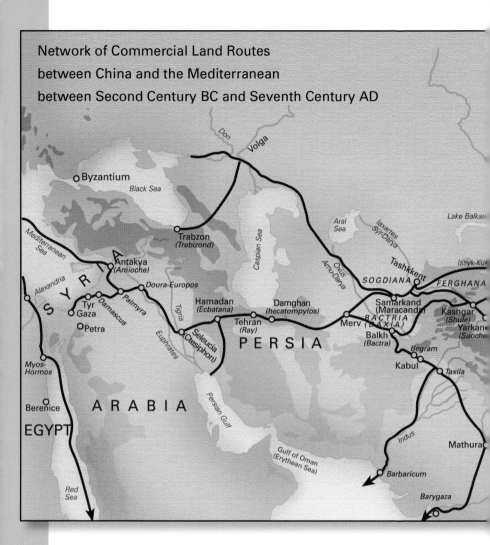

**Network of Commercial Land Routes between China and the Mediterranean between Second Century BC and Seventh Century AD**

The ancient Silk Road, a network of trading routes across Central Asia, started in China and ended beyond the shores of the Mediterranean.

## The Silk Road[8] and Xi'an's Muslim Quarter

The Silk Road is the name given to a route that stretches from Xi'an (then called Chang'an) in Shaanxi province, China to the Mediterranean Coast of the Middle East and beyond to Imperial Rome. It was the principal route in ancient times transporting silk, that most precious of commodities that drove East-West trade.

During the Han dynasty (206 B.C.–A.D. 220), the route began in Xi'an, then the Chinese capital, went northwest into Turkestan and via Kashi (Kashgar) into Afghanistan, and finally through Persia to the Mediterranean — a distance of some 11,265 kilometres (7,000 miles). The route was essentially a series of short caravan journeys linking oases and trading towns.

Traders on the Silk Road used camels, yaks or pack mules to move their goods over these distances. Few of them actually travelled the

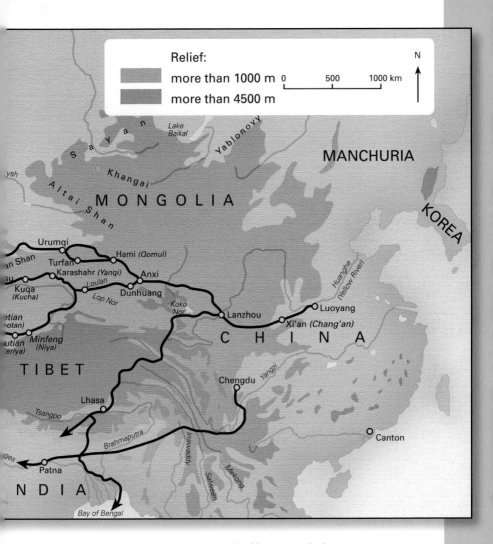

entire route. Instead, they concentrated their efforts on particular routes, leaving other traders to carry goods onward across the other parts of the Silk Road.[9]

Originally founded in A.D. 742, during the Tang dynasty, the Qingzhen Dasi mosque in Xi'an at the Chinese end of the Silk Road was extended and reconstructed in several subsequent dynasties. The present layout of the mosque dates to the 14th century. Amazingly, it suffered little during the Cultural Revolution of the 1960s and '70s. It has a striking Ming dynasty entrance gate, a hall full of ancient furniture, rubbings in Chinese, Arabic and Persian, very fine marquetry and intricate door panelling and a second stone gate with Arabic inscriptions. Turquoise roof tiles and wall reliefs carved from brick decorate the mosque's courtyard. Outside the main prayer hall stands a plaque indicating that it was bestowed on the mosque by the Yongle emperor. Stone steles record the mosque's history in

A Kunming roadside market offers one of the city's delicacies – dried Yunnan ham. Opposite: Women of the Naxi minority group go about their business in a market near Kunming in Yunnan. Below: The maritime Spice Route shows how East and West have been connected through trade on the high seas between the Spice Islands of Indonesia and the markets of Asia and Europe.

Arabic. The minaret in the main courtyard is a beautiful pagoda with green dragons and blue tiles. Beside the imam's quarters is a Qing dynasty map of the Islamic world painted by Chinese Muslims. In the same room is an illuminated handwritten Qing dynasty (1644–1911) Qur'an.

The mosque is one of China's biggest and a large congregation convenes here for Friday prayers. One of Xi'an's ten or so mosques, this is open to visitors between 8.30 a.m. and 6 p.m.

Around the mosques lives Xi'an's strong Muslim community, in old houses that front narrow lanes. The community gradually came to be established in the northwest part of the walled city where about 60,000 live today.

They educate their children in their own primary school, shop at Islamic groceries, eat in Muslim restaurants and observe the fasting month of Ramadan. Xi'an's Muslim residents are easily distinguished from the city's non-Muslims by the white caps they wear and the beards that some of the men keep.[10]

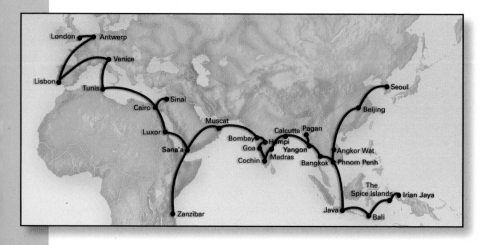

"**I**mperial Decree for Chief Eunuch Zheng He!"

"Zheng He humbly receives the Imperial Decree. Ten thousand years of longevity to Your Gracious Majesty!"

"Now that the Ming Dynasty has firmly entrenched its majestic authority with heavenly blessings, with peace and prosperity prevailing upon the entire Zhong Hua nation, our attention should now turn to the coastal regions and our farther neighbours. The pirates from Japan and other lands have been bothering my loyal subjects and our friendly aliens in the East and South East. Furthermore, for decades now we have not extended our imperial presence and goodwill to the Western Ocean. It is therefore now my explicit wish that the power, prestige and splendour of the Imperial Court be extended once more to the farther shores.

"To expedite this historic mission, I appoint Grand Eunuch Zheng He Commander-in-Chief of the Imperial Expeditions. Details of the mission are herein listed: Go in power, authority and peace. Do justice to the grandeur and splendour of my Dynasty!"

"Zheng He obediently accepts Your Gracious Majesty's Decree with great honour and gratitude. Ten Thousand Years of longevity to Your Gracious Majesty!"

— Kuo Pao Kun, *Descendants of the Eunuch Admiral*

**T**he imposing walls and buildings of Beijing's Forbidden City greet early morning visitors. The completion of the Forbidden City in 1421 coincided with the peak of the voyages of the treasure fleet. The world from China to Africa had been explored, and All Under Heaven acknowledged Yongle, the Son of Heaven.

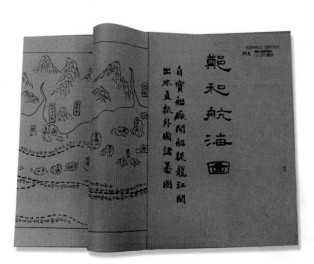

# The Journeys Begin

**T**aicang Harbour, northeast of Shanghai, is the biggest harbour in the Yangzi River. It has the historical distinction of being China's first wharf, the place where thousands of ships gathered. It was also the starting point for Zheng He's voyages. Today, plans are afoot to develop the area into a massive economic and maritime facility that will be part of the Shanghai International Shipping Centre. Construction is in full swing, and one wonders if all traces of the ancient maritime activities that plied these waters might be wiped away as China forges ahead in the 21st century.

**A** woodblock print (opposite) offers a rendition of a treasure ship from Zheng He's fleet. Above: Maps of the voyage taken from the *Wubei Zhi*, a Chinese military treatise compiled in the 17th century.

## Early Shipbuilding

Even before Zhudi issued his edict to build the largest fleet the world had ever seen at the time, China had constructed many imposing maritime armadas. At its height in the 13th century, the Song dynasty navy was an effective fighting force of about 52,000 men serving on board 600 ships. The largest craft was 24 feet (7.3 metres) wide, carried a crew of 42, and was equipped with a whole gamut of weapons, including battering rams, catapults and incendiary devices that could be launched from these catapults.

The average oceangoing civilian Chinese junk in the early 13th century was about 100 feet (30.5 metres) long and 25 feet (7.6 metres) wide and could accommodate a crew of 60 and cargo weighing 120 tons. By the late 13th century, in the Yuan dynasty, the largest junks had a tonnage capacity of 300 tons and carried about 500 to 600 people.[1]

Naval battles in China from the 12th century onwards were mega-affairs. In 1161, the Jin empire in the north attacked the Song capital, Nanjing, in the south with a navy of 600 warships and 70,000 men.[2] In 1274, the great Kublai Khan launched an invasion force from China that included 900 junks, 40,000 men and 15,000 horses. Their target was Japan. They failed. In 1281, they launched an even bigger armada against Japan, with 4,500 ships and 150,000 men. This was the largest fleet ever built in the world until then.[3] They still did not succeed.

On the civilian front, the Chinese had the most formidable fleet of oceangoing junks by the early 13th century, and conducted trade in the Indian Ocean, where previously Arab dhows held sway. During the Yuan dynasty (1271–1368), the Khan sent his fleets to Indonesia, Sri Lanka and India. In Marco Polo's account of China, he claims to have seen at Quanzhou on the Fujian coast oceangoing junks with four masts, 60 individual cabins for merchants and crew capacity of about 300 seamen. So the Chinese were no strangers to fleets that numbered in the thousands, as well as oceangoing junks of pretty vast dimensions.

Different types of ships proliferated, as engineers competed to design ships custom-tailored to carry, among other things, grain, horses, manure, water and even floating banquet halls. Among military craft, there were some ten different warships, ranging from one dubbed the "sea falcon" to the paddle-wheel "flying tiger warship" and the mine-laying articulated barge that could separate in two neat halves and still keep afloat.[4]

## Orders are Issued

If Zhudi's edict to build ships was no great surprise, the scale of its execution might have made his ministers balk. The province of Fujian received orders in May 1403 to build 137 oceangoing ships. In August the same year, the provinces of Jiangsu, Jianxi, Zhejiang, Hunan and Guangdong received orders to construct 200 vessels. Two months later, 188 flat-bottomed transport boats were transformed into oceangoing vessels fit for long journeys on the high seas. In the first three years of Zhudi's reign alone, 1,681 oceangoing ships had been built from scratch or refitted from existing vessels.[5]

To create this massive oceangoing fleet, Zhudi had the Longjiang docks in Nanjing, which already were the largest and most important in China, expanded to twice their original size. They eventually encompassed many square miles on the banks of the Yangzi to

**M**ap of voyages of the treasure fleet taken from the 17th century *Wubei Zhi* or *Treatise on Military Preparations*. The map features coasts and shorelines, ports, islands, reefs and landmarks such as temples and other prominent buildings and structures that can be seen from a boat.

A view of Guangzhou from the 1860s, with the European trading houses operating in the city at the time.

the east of the city. Seven enormous dry docks were built, each connected to the mighty Yangzi by locks and canals, and each dock could accommodate the simultaneous building of three ships.[6] Thus 21 ships could be built at any one time. Yet, it was said, ships were hardly built before another imperial edict was issued demanding more ships.[7] Records indicate that the dry docks were between 90 and 120 feet (27–37 metres) wide. Two docks, however, measured 210 feet (64 metres) wide, and were big enough to accommodate ships with widths of about 160 feet (50 metres).[8]

At the height of shipbuilding activity in the Longjiang docks during Zhudi's reign, twenty to thirty thousand people lived and worked there. These comprised carpenters, sailmakers and shipwrights who had been relocated from various coastal provinces and beyond.

Timber for the ships came from fir, elm, camphor, sophora, cedar, oak, juniper and catalpa trees growing as far away as Annam. To caulk the wood and waterproof the ships, the Chinese used a mixture of cooked tung oil and lime. Thousands upon thousands of tung trees were planted in Nanjing to ensure a ready supply of tung oil.

While some of Zhudi's subjects were busy building ships, others were tasked with manufacturing the goods to be carried on board, including porcelain and silk. Huge quantities of oil, wine, cotton, iron, grain, salt and other essentials were also being produced for the voyages. Each province was designated to produce certain items and the emperor would brook no failure in executing his commands.

# A Close-Up of the Fleet

Historians cannot agree as to the size of a treasure ship. No physical remains exist of any of the ships, so scholars have to rely on existing texts, which may not be accurate. However, the measurements of the dry docks are a good indication of the size of the ships built. Historical records tell us that the *baochuan* (treasure ship) and *longchuan* (dragon ship) were "44 *zhang* 4 *chi* long and 18 *zhang* wide".[9] A *chi* is the Chinese foot and ten *chi* make one *zhang*.

Historians have encountered problems interpreting this figure for the treasure ship because the *chi* was not a uniform length in China. Early interpretations of 44 *zhang* 4 *chi* gave the length of a treasure ship as between 448.8 and 493.5 feet (137 and 150 metres). Since many of the designers of the treasure ships were natives of the coastal Fujian province, it is practical to use the Fujian *chi*, which gives a ship 390 to 408 feet (119–124 metres) long and 160 to 166 feet (49–51 metres) wide. Only in the 19th century would such dimensions be seen again in wooden ships.[10] Many naval historians believe such dimensions for a wooden ship would have made them impossible to sail and so they doubt that these ships were as large as the texts claim.

The design of the treasure ship followed traditional Chinese shipbuilding practices. The *baochuan* had transverse bulkheads that allowed for watertight compartments. The long keel beneath the hull was constructed from long planks bound together by iron hoops. The ships were well balanced because of the keel, the v-shaped hull and the ballast, which was made from uniform cut stones evenly distributed in the lower decks. Holes built into the prow could be filled up during violent storms to help reduce pitching. Floating anchors and large balanced rudders also increased stability in bad weather.

On the main deck rose nine staggered masts and 12 square-shaped red silk sails. Other decks featured luxuriously appointed cabins with windows and balconies. All about the body of the ship were carved or painted auspicious symbols, including phoenixes, dragons and eagles. Fierce dragon eyes were painted on the prow of the *baochuan*.[11]

The *baochuan* wasn't the only type of ship built for this Chinese armada. A 16th century novel based on Zheng He's voyages suggests there were only four *baochuan*: for Zheng He and his three deputies.[12] Records indicate that other types of ships formed the bulk of the treasure fleet. The second-largest boats carried horses, tribute goods and the paraphernalia required for ship-repair at sea. The supply ships ranked next in size and carried food supplies. Next came the troop ships for the soldiers, and then warships and oared patrol boats. Specially built water tankers carried a month's supply of fresh drinking water and were refilled at every stop.[13]

**A**rtist's rendition of a treasure ship. The 600th anniversary celebrations of Zheng He's voyages have seen many attempts to produce models of the treasure ships, aided by depictions of Song, Yuan and Ming ships, as well as historical texts that describe the ships. To date, no physical remains of any ship from the treasure fleet have been discovered.

## People of the Fleet

A wealth of talent sailed on the treasure fleet. There were eunuch ambassadors and imperial representatives, other eunuchs of different ranks, military commanders, regional military commissioners, battalion commanders and company commanders. There were secretaries to check the records and documentation pertaining to grain and fodder supplies, and secretaries to maintain protocol during official receptions of foreign envoys and presentations of Chinese representatives at foreign courts. Astrologers and geomancers kept time, studied the stars and the weather, and observed and interpreted natural phenomena. There were interpreters who spoke Arabic Asian and Central Asian languages, as well as Persian. Medical officers and pharmacologists travelled with the fleet, tasked with gathering herbs and administering to the health of this extraordinary oceangoing community. Then there were the soldiers, sailors and a host of workers involved in specialised ship-repair occupations – the ironsmiths, caulkers, sail builders and scaffolding experts. The treasure ships also carried women aboard, mainly concubines, gifts to the foreign envoys that the treasure fleet was returning home.[14]

In the spring of 1405, more than 300 ships and nearly 28,000 men were ready for the first voyage. The seventh and final voyage 25 years later was as large. The sight of this veritable floating city would have astonished even modern eyes: huge leviathan treasure ships, surrounded by tens of other kinds of ships, the whole cohort awash with tall masts and sails of silk.

As the first ships sailed out of Taicang Harbour and into the ocean, did those watching have any idea that they were on the cusp of a new and magnificent age in history, the age of the treasure fleet?

**T**his 18th century French print marks the different sections of the Forbidden City that hosted foreign envoys and dignitaries.

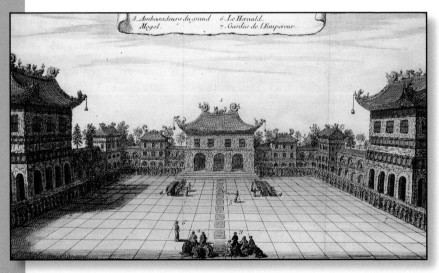

A reconstructed Chinese junk sails out of Taicang Harbour as part of the celebrations commemorating the 600th anniversary of Zheng He's voyages.

# What to See and Do in Taicang

Taicang city in Jiangsu province boasts important Zheng He sites that draw many Zheng He enthusiasts. The most important of these is the Tian Fei temple, or Tian Fei Gong, at which Zheng He and his men prayed before setting out on a voyage. Tian Fei, the Goddess of the Sea, has been revered since the Song dynasty. She was regarded as the protector of Zheng He's fleet. The temple is located in the Liuhe district of the city. Construction began in the 13th century during the Yuan dynasty and the temple subsequently underwent many renovations and repairs.

During Yongle's reign, prayers would be said and rites performed whenever Zheng He's fleet set sail from the harbour. In 1431, on the eve of the last voyage of the treasure fleet, Zheng He erected a plaque in the temple recording Tian Fei's blessings. The crabapple trees growing in the temple grounds are said to have been brought back by Zheng He from one of his voyages.

The temple courtyard houses a memorial to Zheng He — a three-metre tall statue of the admiral and three gigantic wall murals covering 80 square metres. These murals depict Zheng He's fleet leaving Taicang Harbour at the start of its voyages. The artistry of the murals is revealed in the optical illusion that makes the fleet look like it is sailing toward the viewer no matter where the viewer stands in the courtyard.

Other highlights of the temple include a Tian Fei sculpture and a Yuan dynasty gatehouse. There are also graves of one of Zheng He's senior navigators, Zhou Wen, and his wife. Zhou Wen was a Taicang official who sailed with Zheng He on six of the seven voyages. Plaques at the site record his dates of return from each of the six voyages. These tombs were only discovered in 1983 and are of immense historical value.

A monumental Zheng He greets visitors to the Zheng He Park in Kunming, Yunnan.

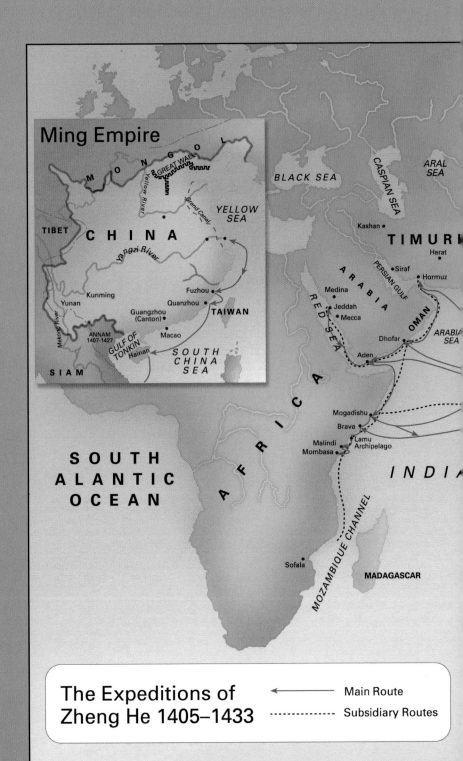

The Expeditions of
Zheng He 1405–1433

⟵ Main Route

------- Subsidiary Routes

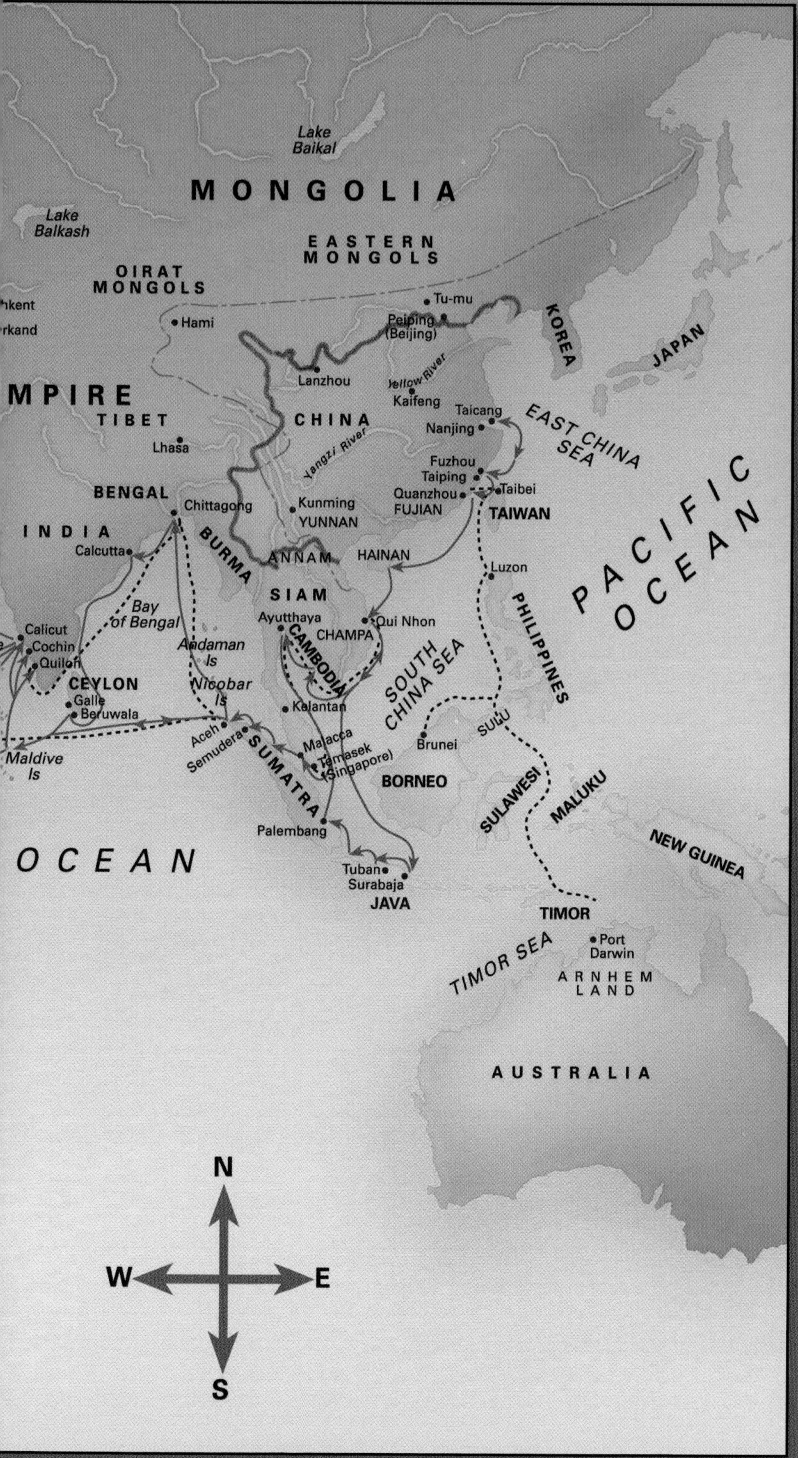
Lake Baikal
MONGOLIA
Lake Balkash
EASTERN MONGOLS
OIRAT MONGOLS
Tu-mu
Hami
Peiping (Beijing)
KOREA
JAPAN
Lanzhou
Yellow River
Kaifeng
MPIRE
TIBET
CHINA
Taicang
Nanjing
EAST CHINA SEA
Lhasa
Yangzi River
Fuzhou
Taiping
Quanzhou
FUJIAN
Taibei
TAIWAN
BENGAL
Chittagong
Kunming
YUNNAN
PACIFIC OCEAN
INDIA
BURMA
ANNAM
HAINAN
Calcutta
Luzon
SIAM
Bay of Bengal
Ayutthaya
Qui Nhon
CHAMPA
PHILIPPINES
Calicut
Cochin
Quilon
Andaman Is
CAMBODIA
SOUTH CHINA SEA
CEYLON
Nicobar Is
Galle
Beruwala
Kelantan
SULU
Aceh
Semudera
Malacca
Tamasek (Singapore)
Brunei
Maldive Is
SUMATRA
BORNEO
SULAWESI
MALUKU
NEW GUINEA
Palembang
OCEAN
Tuban
Surabaja
JAVA
TIMOR
TIMOR SEA
Port Darwin
ARNHEM LAND
AUSTRALIA
N
W
E
S

遊幸江都

# Part Two
# The Voyages

The second Sui emperor Yangdi (A.D. 569–618) prepares to board his vessel. His fleet of sailing craft accompany him. This silk painting is from a history of Chinese emperors published in the 17th century and now kept in the Bibliothèque Nationale in Paris, France. The Chinese already had a strong history of shipbuilding and navigation a thousand years before Zheng He's time.

# Zheng He's Voyages to Southeast Asia

Zheng's He's fleet visited ports in Southeast Asia on all seven voyages. His main port of call in Southeast Asia was Melaka in Malaysia. Other places his fleet is known to have visited include Palembang, Semudera, Deli and Aceh in Sumatra, south Vietnam and Majapahit in Java. The *Ming Shi* (*Official history of the Ming dynasty*) and Fei Xin's and Ma Huan's accounts mention Vietnam (Champa, Panrang, Pulo Condore Islands), Indonesia (Jangala in Java; Palembang, Aru Islands, Semudera, Deli, Lambri, Batak and Pulo Rondo in Sumatra; Geram and Karimata Islands in Indonesian Borneo; and the Sunda Isles, Timor, Belitung and Anambas Island), Brunei, Malaysia (Melaka, Pahang, Kelantan, Langkawi and Sambilang Islands), Thailand and Singapore.

It is difficult to ascertain the modern locations of some of the places mentioned in the accounts. Many of these places were known by old Chinese names, and there is often no archaeological evidence that the fleet ever visited them.

**S**outheast Asia, as depicted in a 16th century map.
Overleaf: A mural in the Klenteng Thiaw Kak Sie in the Javanese town of Cirebon, Indonesia, shows foreign ambassadors paying tribute to the Chinese emperor. This Chinese temple in Cirebon is one of the most beautiful in Java and was constructed in the 17th century. It houses an anchor that allegedly comes from Zheng He's treasure fleet, yet another story surrounding the cult of the Admiral in Southeast Asia.

One day, some way after the great armada entered the Indian Ocean northwest of Sumatra, a terrifying storm came upon his ships. Despite the immensity of his 440-foot command ship, they were thrown into the air like a toy and everyone seemed destined for the bottom of the sea.

"Ah, let us learn from Sang Nila Utama the Prince of Temasek!" And they started to throw everything into the sea including their valuable personal apparel. But no use, the storm persisted, even after the grand eunuchs had also thrown their various headgears into the water.

Usually a very calm leader, Zheng He also began to panic.

"Insya Allah, save us!" he cried out, remembering how he and his family and relatives prayed in his childhood days.

"Ah Buddha, save us!" he appealed, remembering the monk in Xi'an who enlightened him to the holy scriptures.

"Ah Sea Goddess, rescue us!" he prayed, clearly remembering the stone tablets he erected in Taicang and in Changle.

Then a miracle happened. The storm subsided. Not only that, drums and cymbals and chanting were heard from high up in the sky, as an invigorating fragrance filled the air. Suddenly, there appeared on top of the highest mast an angel-like young lady with a graceful face and a youthful body. Her costume and long hair were floating in the air where the storm had altogether lost its trace. And the next morning the lady was gone. People say this was the Sea Goddess herself appearing to calm the hearts and minds of Zheng He and his armada of men.

— Kuo Pao Kun, Descendants of the Eunuch Admiral

# To Melaka, Indonesia and Longyamen

The red brick ruins stand forlornly amid overgrown grass, the fine details of the Indianised carvings on the façades still visible after more than a thousand years. Some structures of these once beautifully decorated temples of a rich and powerful Asian civilisation survived centuries of tropical heat and rain only to be destroyed by bombs during the Vietnam War.

We are in My Son, just outside Da Nang in central Vietnam. Many Vietnamese are unaware of the Hindu-Buddhist Champa civilisation that once flourished in their country and had links to the neigbouring Khmer and distant Javanese cultures. Not so Zheng He and the men of his treasure fleet, which stopped at the modern Vietnamese port of Qui Nhon further south along the coast. To them, Champa was a kingdom rich in precious woods and medicinal aloe. So even though the waters off Champa were pirate-infested, trading at Qui Nhon and re-supplying the treasure ships were well worth the risk.

The imposing façade of St James' Gate (opposite) is all that remains of the 16th century Portuguese fort in Melaka.
Above: A boat anchors off the Thai coastal town of Krabi facing the Indian Ocean. Zheng He's fleet stopped in Thailand on several of the voyages.

## The Nanyang

China's knowledge of the Southern Seas (the Nanhai) and the Southern Ocean (the Nanyang) extends to well before Zheng He's time, to the Han dynasty (206 B.C.–A.D. 220). Merchants of China's southern coasts made a distinction between these entities: the

FORTALEZA DE MALACA.

**M**elaka, a print published in Lisbon, Portugal, in the late 18th century.

Nanhai encompassed the rivers and seas along China's coast and the Pearl River inland delta whereas the Nanyang were the seas around mainland Southeast Asia.

Trade with the countries bordering the Nanyang commenced with the northeast monsoon in December or January. Chinese vessels would leave the customs houses called *hai men* in Guangzhou, Chaozhou and other coastal cities, and sail down the Vietnamese coast and into the Gulf of Siam towards the Malay Peninsula. They would go round the southern tip of the Malay Peninsula and sail up its west coast to Melaka and the Bay of Bengal. In April and May, the southwest monsoon carried the junks from Melaka back along the same route to the southern coast of China.[1]

Thus the Nanyang was always familiar territory to Chinese traders, and the wealth of the region, with its spices, exotic timber and medicinal products, kept bringing Chinese merchants to its shores in the wake of the ever-cyclical monsoon season.

With the voyages of Zheng He's treasure fleet, Southeast Asia, particularly Malaysia and Indonesia, gained importance in relations between China and the region. Indeed, not only has Zheng He been transformed into a god in certain Chinese communities in Southeast Asia, but the very presence of large communities of Chinese in the region could well have had its origins in the extraordinary voyages of Zheng He's treasure fleet.

# Melaka – Emporium of Asia

A spanking new boardwalk lines Melaka's river and a stroll there today gives us a glimpse into both Malaysia's past and its future. Single-storey houses stand on the banks of calm green waters, while here and there the taller structures of graceful pagodas and temples dot the scene. Nearby a Chinese temple with graceful curving eaves and a pair of white cranes on its roof speaks of the country's multi-religious heritage. In the distance skyscrapers of the business district and multi-starred hotels offer a striking contrast to the sense of history that pervades the city.

The 15th century voyages of the treasure fleet coincided with the rise of Melaka, the Malay name for Malacca. This period is often considered the start of Malaysia's recorded history, for Melaka is one of the earliest city-states in the Malay Peninsula.

Facing the southern Strait of Malacca, Melaka is almost at the narrowest point of the strait dividing the Malay Peninsula from the Indonesian island of Sumatra. The city sits at the mouth of the Melaka River and possesses a natural harbour. Add to this the fact that it is where both the southwesterly and northeasterly monsoons meet, and Melaka's rise as a major trading port in the Nanyang was virtually guaranteed. All it needed was some semblance of law and order. Towards the end of the 14th century, Parameswara, a prince from Palembang in Sumatra, decided that Melaka would be the seat of his new capital.[2]

**M**elaka from the sea, when the Dutch occupied the city between 1641 and 1795.

Melaka soon grew into an emporium, a marketplace where commodities such as spices and textiles from all over Southeast Asia could be exchanged for goods from China, India, Persia and the Mediterranean. The Malay Peninsula also provided natural resources such as tin and possibly gold, for it was known in ancient times as the Chersonesus Aurea ("Golden Chersonese" or "Golden Peninsula").

The saying went that whoever controlled Melaka had Venice in its grip. The city came to be known throughout the Indian Ocean and beyond for its amazing commercial wealth. It excited the interest of the Siamese kingdom in the north, as well as Sumatran states, all of which coveted Melaka's rising influence. Parameswara knew only too well that Melaka needed the protection of a polity that could keep both the Siamese and Sumatran princes in check. Enter Zheng He and his treasure fleet …

While the situation thus simply described may not give the full complexity of the relationship between Melaka and the surrounding powers during its early years, we do know that relations between China and Melaka were extremely close.

Parameswara had made a trip to China in 1405 for the purpose of offering tribute to the Yongle emperor and placing himself under the protection of the Dragon Throne. Yongle granted him a seal that declared Melaka an independent kingdom. Parameswara later received more seals from Zheng He when the treasure fleet called at Melaka on its third voyage from China.

The Yongle emperor dictated a special dedication that was inscribed on a stone stele. In it, the emperor explained that it was to his deceased father's "overflowing favour and good blessings" that Melaka owed its peace and prosperity, and how happy he was that Melaka desired "to be treated as a subject state of the Middle Kingdom in order to excel and be distinguished from the barbarian domains".[3]

The emperor also composed a poem for the occasion "to be engraved on everlasting stone, forever to show your descendants and the people of ten thousand generations to come that this bond with the Middle Kingdom shall be there like heaven unto the end of time".[4] With these close ties to China, Melaka ensured its safety from the Siamese and Sumatrans.

Of course China's interest in Melaka lay in its position at the entrance to the Indian Ocean. It was the ideal location for the treasure fleet to stock up on supplies en route to Sri Lanka and India, as well as on the return journey from the Indian Ocean to the Chinese coast. The chronicler Ma Huan indicates in his writings that Chinese artisans from the treasure fleet built warehouses and granaries in Melaka specifically to house supplies for the treasure fleet.[5]

The Chinese found an infinite variety of goods in Melaka, including spices from the spice islands of the Moluccas in the eastern

**A** map of Melaka in 1630, a decade before the Dutch captured the city. It forms part of a compilation of Portuguese maps detailing Portugal's far-flung maritime empire.

Indonesian archipelago, pearls, feathers of exotic birds, rare woods, aloes and exquisite batik textiles.

The bridge leads onto Melaka's famous Jonker Street in this 19th century print.

Ma Huan gives us fascinating insights into the beliefs of the people of Melaka. There was an animistic belief that even an inanimate object possessed a soul that had to be appeased before undertaking activity associated with it. And a belief that if a woman died in childbirth, her spirit took the form of a terrifying head with entrails and attacked infants.[6] He also recounted the belief in were-people like "black tigers … with dark stripes" who turned into ordinary people when they visited towns.[7] Interestingly, this belief persists in Malaysia today in some villages on the fringe of forests.

## Melaka's Chinese Heritage

I watch keenly, fascinated by the deft strokes that encrust the glossy black wood with tiny flecks of gold. Quickly the gold leaf brings to life the beautifully carved Chinese calligraphy that speaks of abundant prosperity and wealth. I am at one of the few Chinese sign-making shops in Melaka, witnessing an amazing skill that has been handed down from generation to generation.

Fei Xin, another of Zheng He's chroniclers, writes in his book *Xing cha sheng lan* (*Marvellous visions from the star raft*) that Malays possessed skin like black lacquer, "but there were white-skinned people among them who are of Chinese descent."

That Melaka had a large Chinese community is evident in the historical Chinese quarter called Bukit Cina, said to have been established to house a Chinese princess's retinue of five hundred people. Her arrival in Melaka is quite a story.

During the reign of Melaka's second sultan, Mansur Shah, in the 1460s, a Chinese junk arrived filled with delicate gold needles and a message from the Chinese emperor: "For every gold needle, I have a subject; if you could count their number, then you would know my power." The sultan sent back a ship of sacks of tiny sago grains and the message: "If you can count the grains of sago on this ship you will have guessed the number of my subjects correctly, and you will know my power." Impressed, the Chinese emperor sent his daughter to marry the sultan.[8]

Chinese records do not corroborate this story although Portuguese records (Melaka became a Portuguese colony in 1511) relate the marriage of the second sultan of Melaka to "the daughter of the king of China's captain". Chinese captains, or *kapitan*, were appointed by the Portuguese to oversee Melaka's Chinese community.

The Chinese cemetery in Bukit Cina has some ancient tombstones, a few dating to the Ming period. In the grounds of the Sam Po Kong, a temple built at the foot of Bukit Cina in 1795 and dedicated to Zheng He, is a well said never to run dry. This is Sultan's Well or Perigi Rajah, and it is dedicated to Princess Hang Li Poh. Zheng He is believed to have drunk from it and caused the purity of the water to increase. Many devotees make the journey here to pray to the eunuch admiral who has become a god to them.

# What to See and Do in Melaka

## Cheng Hoon Teng and Sam Po Kong

Cheng Hoon Teng takes pride of place as the oldest Chinese temple in Malaysia. It was built in 1646, supposedly with material specifically shipped from China. The temple, which follows the arrangement of a typical temple of south China, is dedicated to Kuan Yin, the Goddess of Mercy. It is always busy, with devotees arriving at all hours to light joss sticks, pray and make offerings. Sam Po Kong in Bukit Cina is another important temple in Melaka and is dedicated to the intrepid voyager Zheng He. A must-see for Zheng He buffs.

## Cheng Ho Cultural Museum

Melaka will soon see the Cheng Ho Cultural Museum, which is being built on the site of the large Chinese *guan chang*, or depot, that was used as a storehouse for the treasure fleet. Some of the buildings on the present site originated in the 16th and 17th centuries, when they were used by the Chinese *kapitan*, or superintendants, who were put in charge of the Chinese community by the Portuguese and Dutch rulers. Through multimedia and interactive exhibits, this state-of-the-art museum offers visitors a glimpse into the activities of the treasure fleet in Melaka. It is located at 51, Lorong Hang Jebat. Check ahead on its opening: (606) 282-5588 (phone), (606) 281-5588 (fax) or infoexchange@chengho.org

## Jonker Street

"Jonker" is Dutch for "second-class gentleman". This is one of Melaka's most famous shopping streets, an antique collector's paradise for anything from brass lamps and Victorian clocks to traditional Melakan furniture, jewellery, opium beds, and Ming and Song dynasty porcelain. Look out also for the huge array of Malaysian handicrafts, and pop into Chinese shops selling carved and painted Chinese signs and order special pieces of Chinese calligraphy.

Chinese porcelain has been recovered from wrecks in Southeast Asian waters.

## Melaka's Colonial Buildings

Melaka's colonisation by three European nations has given it a legacy of well-preserved monuments. Chief among them is the 15th century A Famosa, a Portuguese fort, of which only the main gate, St James' Gate, remains. The Dutch superimposed their coat of arms above the gate. Only the walls remain of another building from the Portuguese era, St Paul's Church (1521). Melaka's Town Square preserves its Dutch heritage in the mid-17th century Stadthuys, or City Hall, once the administrative seat of the Dutch colonial government, and today the Museum of History and Ethnography. The Dutch also built Christ Church, Malaysia's oldest Protestant church, which still serves Melaka's Anglican community. The British erected the Queen Victoria Fountain in 1904 to commemorate the queen's diamond jubilee.

Melaka is famous for producing tiny shoes. Binding the feet and wearing such shoes was a custom of elite women in China during the Qing dynasty.

Restored Peranakan shophouse in Melaka featuring European and Asian influences.

## Peranakans

A unique community living in Melaka goes by different names: Baba-Nyonya, Peranakan, Straits Chinese. Their culture is a blend of Chinese and Malay customs. Some say the Peranakan community in Melaka originated with the arrival of the legendary Princess Hang Li Poh in the 15th century.

Peranakan women, called Nyonyas, wear traditional Malay *kebaya* embroidered with Chinese motifs and have a penchant for beautiful silver jewellery that shows both Chinese and Middle Eastern influence. Peranakans speak a patois called Baba Malay, a mixture of Chinese and Malay dialects.

Jalan Tun Tan Cheng Lok has some immaculately restored Peranakan homes decorated with ornate tiles. Some of them have been converted into boutique hotels. The Baba-Nyonya Heritage Museum on the same street is the best place to get an insight into the Peranakan lifestyle. Peranakan food, sold in many places, is not to be missed.

Wooden clogs lie on colourful tiled steps leading up to a traditional Peranakan shophouse in Melaka.

## Melaka's Maritime Museum

The Maritime Museum in Melaka takes the appropriate form of a ship moored in the harbour! This is a replica of the Portuguese *Flor de la Mar* that sank in 1511 in the Malacca Strait, some say with 60 tons of gold. On board are models of ships that called at Melaka's harbour from the 14th century onwards. The museum opens from 9 in the morning until 6 in the evening.

# The Treasure Fleet in Indonesia

The green hills of Penggiling are a romantic backdrop to the Klenteng Sam Po Kong in Semarang on the northern coast of central Java in Indonesia. Their verdant hue makes a lovely contrast to the bright red roof tiles of this temple devoted to Zheng He, or Sam Po, the name by which he is worshipped here in Indonesia. Quite extraordinarily, the eunuch admiral has become a Southeast Asian deity. His birthday is celebrated each year at this Semarang temple, when thousands honour his spirit with exhuberant drumming and lion dancing.

Legend has it that one of Zheng He's ships was wrecked off the coast of Semarang and the anchor in the temple came from it. The anchor looks modern and its design is European, for it came off a Dutch ship of a much later period. Other legends abound. One of Zheng He's ship officers is believed to have settled in Semarang and founded a temple. His burial site in a cave is a place of pilgrimage and the centre of the Sam Po Kong in Semarang. The spiritual hold of the treasure fleet is very much in evidence in modern-day Semarang, and ordinary believers come with great faith to pray at the temple for their wishes to be granted.

On each of the seven voyages to the Indian Ocean, the treasure fleet sailed through the Indonesian archipelago, with its thousands of islands. The major islands of Sumatra and Java had by the early 15th century developed their own indigenous kingdoms of Majapahit (13th to 15th centuries) and Sri Vijaya (7th to 10th centuries), which observed Hindu and Buddhist customs.

**A**n early 17th century Portuguese map of Aceh on the northern tip of the Indonesian island of Sumatra.

**A**n 18th century print of Batavia shows the old harbour Sunda Kelapa, as well as the fine Dutch buildings and churches that are now part of Jakarta's colonial quarter.

Islam was also beginning to make inroads in the region, introduced by Arab, Persian and Gujerati traders who brought European, Indian and Western Asian goods to Southeast Asia and returned to their native lands laden with produce from the Indonesian archipelago and China.

The sheer vastness of the island archipelago meant that many individual states had opportunities to advance in political and commercial influence, and they jostled each other for power. Into this potent mix sailed the treasure fleet, to add to the political complexity of the region.

Palembang, an important Sumatran city-state in the early 15th century, lay upriver from the northern coast of the island facing the Malacca Strait. Relations between the region and China dated back to at least the 11th century. In the late 14th and early 15th centuries, Palembang tried to enlist Chinese help against neighbouring Java. A series of wars between the two weakened Palembang to the point that it was taken over by a Chinese pirate, Chen Zuyi, a few years before Zheng He's fleet arrived in Sumatra in 1406.[9] Zheng He didn't stop in Palembang then, but on his return journey to China in 1407, he deposed the pirate king in a naval battle[10] that reduced piracy in the region for a while.

Another north Sumatran state, Semudera, saw Chinese military intervention in 1414, when Zheng He supported one political faction at the expense of the other, and carried the losing claimant to the throne back to China for execution.[11]

Javanese coastal towns, including Sunda Kelapa (Jakarta), Cirebon, Semarang, Tuban and Gresik (near Surabaya), benefited from the increased trading relations between China and Java during this time, and many of these towns grew large on the back of sizeable Chinese communities.

Ma Huan's writings provide some information about Indonesian practices, including the Hindu ritual *suttee*, where the living wife of a dead man jumps into his funeral pyre and is cremated alive. He also recorded the storytelling traditions of the Javanese and noted that populations of Chinese lived in areas visited by the treasure fleet.[12] These included Gresik on the northwestern coast of Java, which was governed by a man from Guangdong, and nearby Surabaya. It is clear from his writings that these areas had large communities of Chinese during Zheng He's time, and the trading that the treasure fleet encouraged could have given rise to increased emigration from China.

# What to See and Do in Indonesia

## Jakarta

Jakarta, the capital of Indonesia on the north coast of West Java, has a population of over 12 million people. The historic heart of the old Dutch quarter is Taman Fatahillah (Fatahillah Square). The Museum of the History of Jakarta occupies the old City Hall, which was built in 1710. The building is an excellent example of Dutch architecture and it showcases Jakarta's colonial history as the Dutch city of Batavia. Other historical buildings around the square include the Wayang Museum, with its collection of traditional Indonesian shadow puppets, and the Balai Seni Rupa, or Fine Arts Museum. Wander around the square to see more examples of Dutch colonial architecture. Stop for a coffee at the Grand Salon of Café Batavia, which dates from the early 19th century and is made from beautiful old teakwood.

South of Taman Fatahillah is Glodok, Jakarta's Chinatown. This area is a maze of narrow streets filled with hawkers, foodstalls and small shops, all with discernible Chinese architectural features.

Dharma Jaya Temple on Jalan Petak Sembilan, founded in the 1650s and dedicated to the Chinese goddess of mercy, Kuan Yin, is one of the earliest centres of worship for the Batavian Chinese. There are also mosques for Glodok's Chinese Muslims, whose ancestors converted to Islam when they arrived in Indonesia. The Kebun Jeruk Mosque in Jalan Hayam Wuruk was built in 1786 and its architecture is a mix of Islamic and Chinese styles. Another 18th century Chinese mosque is the Mesjid Krukut in Jalan Kebahagiaan, off Jalan Gajah Mada.

In Jakarta there is a Sam Po temple dedicated to Zheng He. The Ancol *klenteng*, or temple, in the area of Tanjung Priok, east Jakarta,

An Indonesian Chinese man burns joss sticks at a shrine inside Jakarta's Klenteng Ancol, one of the city's most well known Chinese temples.

SAGAM INAYAH

The sleek and colourful prows of traditional *pinisis* line the old harbour at Sunda Kelapa in Jakarta. Opposite: A cycle-drawn cart passes near the Tay Kak Sie Chinese temple in Semarang's Chinatown.

has Islamic tombs that are supposedly those of one of Zheng He's ship officers, his Sundanese wife and her father. The temple has within its sacred setting both Islamic and Daoist-Buddhist spaces for worship, and adherents of both faiths come to pay their respects. The main deity is a Daoist god of riches, while to the left of the main altar is the Zheng He altar and a statue that represents the great admiral himself. This temple was erected in the mid-17th century, and a stone inscription from the early 20th century dates its founding to the end of the Ming dynasty.

Sunda Kelapa, the old harbour of Jakarta, is also worth a visit for a glimpse into the city's maritime history. Here, old wooden schooners called *pinisis* sail gracefully in and out of port, carrying timber from Indonesia's forest-rich Kalimantan and Sulawesi regions.

The nearby Museum Bahari or Maritime Museum is an important 18th century building. It was originally used as a warehouse to store spices. Part of the exterior of the museum boasts the only remaining portion of Jakarta's old city wall. Inside the museum, exhibits detail the country's maritime history through ship models and photographs. The museum is open daily and an admission fee is payable.

## Semarang

Semarang in central Java boasts Tay Kak Sie temple, an important Chinese temple that was constructed at the end of the 18th century. It is from this temple in the centre of Semarang's Chinatown that Zheng He devotees process to the famous cave temple called Gedung Batu.

Locals believe that Gedung Batu was set up by Zheng He's master pilot, and an old Muslim tomb inside the cave is said to be

**F**açade of Semarang's Sam Po Kong.

his final resting place. So strong is the devotion to Zheng He that it has been extended to Zheng He's ship officers, whom locals believe helped spread Islam in Java. An anchor from a 19th century Dutch ship is also venerated, the devotees holding fast to the belief that this is an anchor from one of Zheng He's original ships.

Both Muslims and Chinese worship within the stone walls of this cave temple. Major celebrations take place here on the 29th day of the sixth lunar month, when the most famous procession from Tay Kak Sie to Gedung Batu takes place. Smaller ceremonies are held at Gedung Batu twice a month.

Whether or not Zheng He actually visited Semarang, the devotion to his cult is as strong here as it is at the other Javanese ports he is known to have visited.

**O**fferings of drink lie next to a bronze urn inside the Tay Kak Sie temple in Semarang.

## Surabaya and Tuban

Zheng He's fleet visited Surabaya and Tuban in Java in the 15th century, as well as Gresik, which lies very close to Surabaya. Today, Gresik is an industrial town, while nearby Surabaya is Indonesia's second largest city.

Surabaya has been an important port since the 16th century. Although not a popular tourist destination, it has some interesting sites, among them the Kali Mas, or River of Gold. This is a wharf where traditional Indonesian *pinisis* are moored. Many of these vessels are Bugis schooners, still built in the traditional way without nails, using a series of hooks made of ironwood to bind the hull together beneath the waterline.

Surabaya's Arab quarter is also worth a visit for its distinctive old world charms. A Chinese temple lies not far from the Arab quarter.

This is the Hok An Kiong in Surabaya's Chinatown, said to be about three hundred years old.

Surabaya boasts a modern building that transports visitors back to the time of the admiral. The Sam Po Kong or Sam Po Tae Jin along Jalan Demak has an anchor and a six metre long beam that is supposed to have come from one of Zheng He's ships. It even has pictures of the admiral's birth place and a statue of him. Although built almost entirely in Chinese temple style, the building functions as a mosque and is open to all faiths.

Tuban, west of Surabaya on the north coast of East Java, was established in the 12th century and was an important trading port in the 16th century, with a large community of Chinese merchants. Significant quantities of Chinese ceramics have been found in the area. One of the largest Chinese temples in East Java is located in Tuban. This is the Klenteng Kwan Sing Bio, whose main entrance is adorned by dragon carvings.

**T**he Klenteng Thiaw Kak Sie in Cirebon.

## Cirebon

A five-hour drive east of Jakarta brings you to the coastal town of Cirebon, where stories of Zheng He remind visitors just how important the admiral continues to be. One legend has Zheng He fighting and killing a snake off the Cirebon coast. He killed it by taking its pearl and a rocky island appeared in the sea at this great feat of strength.

The Thiaw Kak Sie in Cirebon houses an anchor that residents believe comes from one of Zheng He's ships. The 17th century temple is beautifully maintained and the ornate gilded roof is painted with brightly coloured dragons and other mythical beasts.

**T**he Mesjid Agung or Grand Mosque in Cirebon is built entirely out of wood.

# Longyamen and Singapore

Singapore's place in the voyages of Zheng He's fleet is slightly enigmatic. It is the only country in Southeast Asia with a Chinese majority. It lies at the very tip of the Malay Peninsula, and the treasure fleet certainly would have had to pass by to get from the South China Sea into the Malacca Strait. Did it stop at Singapore on one of its seven voyages?

Local historians debating this issue are looking in particular at a place called Longyamen, mentioned in Zheng He's maps. Literally translated from the Chinese, it means dragon's teeth gate. Interestingly enough, there were rock formations in Singapore's Keppel Harbour that resembled two long "teeth" sticking out of the water. These formations were dynamited in the 19th century by the British after they founded Singapore in 1819. Was this the reason the name Longyamen came about? If so, is Keppel Harbour Longyamen? Some believe that Longyamen is Singapore.

Whatever the case, Singapore is a must-see on any visitor's Southeast Asian travel itinerary. The island's pre-colonial past is very evident in Fort Canning, a leafy hill not far from the Singapore River, where archaeological excavations have uncovered 14th and 15th century remains of a royal Malay palace. The notion that Singapore was always the sleepy coastal village that Raffles saw in 1819 is rapidly being dismissed, and ancient remains show that the country was very much linked to the regional and international trade routes of the Malay archipelago and all the power struggles that that entailed.

# What to See and Do in Singapore

## Fort Canning, Empress Place and Parliament House[13]

While there is no documentation to suggest that Zheng He's fleet actually landed in Singapore, there is a wealth of archaeological evidence from the island republic to confirm that it has been inhabited from at least the early 14th century. Excavations at Fort Canning hill have turned up ancient brick ruins and Chinese porcelain from the first half of the 14th century. The finds corroborate Malay legends that speak of an old palace atop the hill.

An Islamic grave dedicated to Iskander Shah, a sultan from the Melaka sultanate of the 15th century, can be found on the hill. Although this ceremonial tomb dates from the early 19th century, there is enough archaeological evidence to suggest that it is built on

**A**rtist's impression of Longyamen, or Dragon's Teeth Gate, before it was dynamited in the 19th century. Longyamen is mentioned in the *Wubei Zhi* charts that document Zheng He's voyages. Scholars believe it was located in the waters off today's Labrador Park on the west coast of Singapore.

**A** statue of Stamford Raffles, founder of modern Singapore, stands close to the Asian Civilisations Museum at Empress Place. The island republic that he founded in 1819 and made a free port is consistently one of the busiest ports in the world (opposite).

the ruins of a 14th century brick structure. In 1928, 14th-century-style gold ornaments were found on top of the hill during construction to build a small reservoir.

Excavations at Empress Place, close to the Asian Civilisations Museum, revealed yet more evidence of the early phase of Singapore's history. Finds include Chinese porcelain that dates from the late 13th to mid-15th centuries. Construction work at the site of the new Parliament House also revealed pre-colonial artefacts that had lain undisturbed for the last 500 years. Again, Chinese porcelain shards formed part of the finds, this batch dating from the late 13th to the early 15th centuries.

## Asian Civilisations Museum

This museum, with two separate buildings about 20 minutes apart on foot, one at Empress Place and the other at Armenian Street, is an absolute gem. The imposing European colonial structure at Empress Place was constructed in the late 1800s as an administrative hub for local government. The museum there showcases the ancient civilisations of West, South, Southeast and East Asia with exhibits that are as informative as they are evocatively lit. The soaring ceilings of the ten galleries across three floors lend both intimacy and a sense of spaciousness.

The Armenian Street branch of the Asian Civilisations Museum occupies another charming 19th century building, the Tao Nan School, the first school in Singapore to use Mandarin as the language of instruction. The building's beautifully restored façade consists of arches and colonnades, while the cool interior offers visitors fascinating displays, particularly on Peranakan culture, that unique blend of Chinese and Malay ethnicities which traces its origins to Melaka and Penang.

Both branches open Monday (12–6 p.m.), Tuesday to Sunday except Friday (9 a.m.–6 p.m.) and Friday (9 a.m.–9 p.m.).

## Boat Quay and Clarke Quay

Singapore River near the waterfront is the best place to savour the island's maritime past. Along Boat Quay and Clarke Quay, restored shophouses and godowns stand testimony to the hustle and bustle of early traders who flocked to the free port of Singapore to sell their goods.

The hustle and bustle continues today in the form of flocks of tourists who throng the bars and restaurants that offer al fresco riverside dining. You can also take river cruises in water taxis, junks or bumboats, to sail under 19th century whitewashed bridges and marvel at the elegant skyscrapers that dominate the island's dynamic central business district. At night, bright lights from this nocturnal wining and dining hub turn the area into a magical fantasyland.

## Chinatown

The Chinatown area offers the visitor a glimpse into the heart of Chinese Singapore, with its busy alleyways, covered footpaths, restored shophouses and religious and cultural buildings. The Chinese Opera Teahouse in Smith Street allows tourists to relax as they sip

**S**ingapore's dramatic skyline of skyscrapers and restored colonial buildings.

from a wide range of Chinese teas. Weekends, visitors can sample traditional Chinese fare while listening to Chinese opera.

Along South Bridge Road are shops selling traditional Chinese medicine. The Jamae Mosque and the Hindu Sri Mariamman Temple are located here, testifying to Singapore's multicultural life.

The Tzu Chi Foundation in Trengganu Street nearby used to be a Chinese opera house. Responding to a changing clientele, it now houses souvenir shops and antique dealers on the ground floor. A short distance away, a Chinatown complex features a basement that offers traditional Chinese hawker food, while the Chinatown Heritage Centre in Pagoda Street authentically recreates living conditions of 19th century Chinese immigrants who set up home in Chinatown, from narrow dingy staircases to the cramped rooms and communal kitchens.

The best way to appreciate Chinatown is to spend three or four hours simply wandering about or sitting in the many coffee shops to watch the busy street life and admire the traditional shophouse architecture.

The restored Thian Hock Keng temple in Singapore's Chinatown is the island's oldest and most important Hokkien temple. Dating from the 1840s, it is dedicated to Ma Zu, the Goddess of the Sea and Protector of Sailors.

## Arab Street and Kampong Glam

This area in the vicinity of Victoria Street and Rochor Road was first settled by Arab traders in the early 19th century. Kampong Glam became a focal point for the Malay community, with the convenient presence of mosques and businesses and stores catering to Malay tastes. In Arab Street, you can pick up a large variety of colourful silks, brocades, batiks and handicrafts at reasonable prices.

The nearby Sultan Mosque, with a beautiful golden dome and minarets, is the largest mosque in Singapore. It was completed in 1928, built on the site of another mosque built in 1824, five years after the founding of Singapore. Visitors are allowed outside of prayer times, but you need to dress appropriately and leave your footwear at the door.

Another mosque in the area worth visiting is the Malabar Jamal-ath Mosque next to the old Malay cemetery along Victoria Street. This blue and gold mosque was built for the Indian Muslim community, hence the name Malabar, which refers to the Malabar Coast in southwestern India. The cemetery has tombs dating to the first half of the 19th century.

## Little India

Serangoon Road has come to be known as Little India in Singapore, not only because this is the place that the first Indian immigrants to the island set up home, but also because the Indian character of the locale has survived right up to the present. Here you will find Indian restaurants chock-full of authentic Indian food, especially South

Indian vegetarian cuisine; Hindu temples ornately decorated with colourful reliefs and sculptures; and shops selling spices, flowers, saris and all things Indian.

Campbell Lane, Little India Arcade and Clive Street, all off Serangoon Road, are well worth a walk through to sample the sights, sounds and smells of Little India. In October or November, during Deepavali, the Hindu celebration of the triumph of light over darkness, the whole of Little India is lighted up with thousands of coloured lights.

Hindu temples in the area include the Sri Veeramakaliamman Temple in Belilios Road and the Sri Srinivasa Perumal Temple near Perumal Road, both dating from around the mid-1800s.

**S**ultan Mosque in Singapore's Kampong Glam was built in the early 19th century and subsequently restored. The original structure was partially financed by the East India Company that had founded Singapore.

# Zheng He's Voyages to Sri Lanka and India

Calicut, today's Kozhikode on India's southwestern coast in the state of Kerala, was not always as sleepy as it appears. It was a great trading city in Zheng He's day and the treasure fleet visited Calicut on all seven of its voyages. Quilon and Cochin were also important states in Kerala at the time, and Zheng He's fleets called on both cities several times. The fleet also visited Sri Lanka on each voyage, located as it is along the way to India. Other places the admiral's ships visited include Bengal and Tamil Nadu to the east of the Indian subcontinent. The first giraffe to arrive in China came from Bengal in 1414, a gift from the ruler who in turn had received it as a gift from the king of Malindi in East Africa.

**T**his map of Sri Lanka (Ceylon) and the Coromandel and Malabar coasts of India was produced in 1733 by German mapmakers Homann Erben. The founder Johann Homann was imperial geographer to the Holy Roman Emperor Charles VI (*r.* 1711–40).

"Hey! Hoi! Good people there. Where have we come to? What do you call this beautiful land of yours here?"

"Oh, this is the land where the Buddha walked, where the Buddha bathed, where the Buddha slept. This is the jewel of the world, the jewel formed by a drop of the Buddha's tear."

Zheng He and members of his fleet were overcome with joy. Is this the promised land of abundance and tolerance where men are free to work and live, the land where there is only justice and no reign of terror?

Maybe, because they said this was the place where Adam made a mountain and Adam is the brother of Pan Gu, and both Adam and Pan Gu are ancestors of men.

— Kuo Pao Kun, Descendants of the Eunuch Admiral

A Buddhist monk stands in a doorway of the Malwatte Vihara, a temple in Kandy, central Sri Lanka. Historical records from both Sri Lanka and China document the activities of the treasure fleet in Sri Lanka, especially their political and military exploits.

# To Sri Lanka and India's Spice Coast

**5**

**V**isitors to Sri Lanka have often raved about the beauty of this Indian Ocean island, a giant pearl drop descending from the tip of the Indian subcontinent. Its beautiful beaches, lush forests and landscapes have given rise to all kinds of epithets for the island, with some even describing it as the site of the biblical Garden of Eden.

It's easy to see why: sailing upon the pale blue waters of the northern reaches of the Indian Ocean, the first sight of Sri Lanka is a long, green line of tropical palms, set off by sparkling white beaches, some of them voted among the most beautiful in the world. Unawatuna, Hikkaduwa and Bentota offer the quintessential sun and surf experience, while waters off the coastlines teem with rare corals and brilliantly coloured tropical fish.

Just beyond the swaying palms grow jungles rich in rivers and waterfalls. Located at the southeastern tip of the country is the Yala West National Park, one of Sri Lanka's most famous nature reserves. Within its leafy confines roam elephants, wild boars and even leopards. High in the tree canopy, the shrill calls of birds and monkeys pierce the dense jungle air and add to the primeval atmosphere. Even after December 2004, in the aftermath of the tsunami tragedy, the natural beauty of this remarkable island's coastline is undeniable.

Zheng He and his fellow voyagers experienced firsthand this incredibly beautiful natural landscape.

**A** toddy tapper (opposite) swings between coconut trees at sunset on a Sri Lankan beach. Above: A Portuguese cannon points to the Indian Ocean from the historic fort of Galle in southern Sri Lanka.

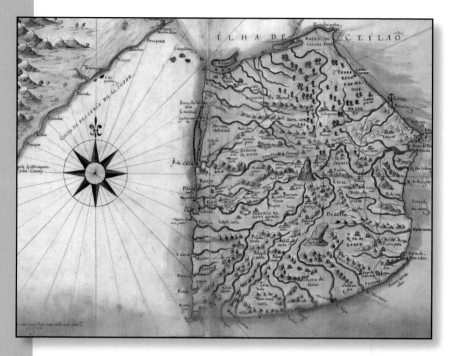

Portuguese map of Sri Lanka from the early 17th century with details of rivers, settlements, forests and mountains, including Adam's Peak, shown here in the centre of the map.

The scribes of the treasure fleet recorded much information about Sri Lanka, including its great wealth and the importance of religion to the people. Sri Lanka already had a complex multi-religious, multi-ethnic society that showcased its illustrious history stretching back to the time of the Hindu epic *Ramayana*. Of its richness, it was said each time it rained, rubies, sapphires and topaz washed down the slopes of Adam's Peak, a sacred mountain in the centre of island.[1]

## Intrigue and the Sacred Tooth

The treasure fleet returned to Sri Lanka on its third voyage from China, this time bringing an extraordinary stone tablet carved in Chinese, Tamil and Persian. Dated 15 February 1409, the tablet was intended as a gift to the king of Sri Lanka. On it were inscribed praises to the Buddha in Chinese, to the Hindu God Tenavarai-Nayanar in Tamil and to Allah in Persian. It was clear that Zheng He was fully aware of the complex religious make-up of the island.

Accompanying the tablet were "gold and silver, gold-embroidered jewelled banners of variegated silk, incense-burners and flower-vases, silks of many colours in lining and exterior, lamps and candles with other gifts in order to manifest the high honour of the Lord Buddha", as well as gifts to the other two religious deities in exactly the same quantities.[2]

At the time the island was divided into three states, each vying for supremacy. The tablet-bearing visitors found themselves caught in the very thick of three warring factions: the main Singhalese ruler with his seat in Kotte in the centre of the island, the Hindu Tamil rulers in the north, and a Muslim leader who wanted to establish Islam as the main religion on the island. Added to this potent mix was an ambitious upstart, Alakeswara, who wanted to wrest power from the Kotte king. He had already gained a hero's reputation, having defeated a Tamil invasion from the north, and was eager for more.

How it came about that Alakeswara was recorded as receiving Zheng He on his arrival is not known. But what has come down to us is the story of how Alakeswara refused to pay tribute to the Ming emperor or to erect the trilingual stone tablet.[3] Instead, in a brief skirmish, he drove the Chinese back to their ships. The Sinhalese and Chinese accounts differ on what happened next.

The official Ming history, the *Ming shi lu*, states that when the Chinese boats returned to Sri Lanka, Alakeswara sent his son to demand tribute. When Zheng He refused, some fifty thousand Sinhalese troops descended upon the boats to seize them. Unable to return to the ships because his way had been blocked by the advancing troops, Zheng He turned back towards the city and, with the few soldiers accompanying him, succeeded in capturing Alakeswara, whom he quickly spirited away. He returned to the ships, which by then had been deserted by the Sri Lankan troops who had raced back to the capital upon news of Alakeswara's capture.

The *Ming shi lu* then states that Zheng He took Alakeswara all the way back to Nanjing, where the Yongle emperor finally pardoned him.[4] The record is confused at this point whether it was in fact

**M**ural in the Temple of the Tooth in Kandy, central Sri Lanka, depicting the return of the relic to the temple.

**A**n old Portuguese map shows the eastern Sri Lankan town of Mannar.

the legitimate Sinhalese king who had been brought to China, or Alakeswara, or both.

The Chinese tradition, though, states just how extraordinarily brave and clever Zheng He and his men were to have outsmarted the Sri Lankans, who are described in other records as "noxious pests", "insignificant worms, deserving to die ten thousand times over". In somewhat over the top terms, the actions of the Chinese troops were thus described:

*Straight-away, their dens and hideouts we ravaged,*
*And made captive that entire country,*
*Bringing back to our august capital,*
*Their women, children, families, and retainers, leaving not one.*[5]

The Sinhalese account is tinged with political machinations and is bound up with the island's fierce sense of independence. In it, Alakeswara enters into an alliance with Zheng He, who captures the Sinhalese King Vijaya Bahu IV when the king arrives at Alakeswara's palace to receive Zheng He's tablet. It is Vijaya Bahu IV who gets taken to China and is later released by the Yongle emperor.[6]

These narratives honouring their respective heroes are a fascinating insight into relations between two very different countries in the early 15th century, each bent on preserving their sovereignty and prestige.

One Ming account mentions Zheng He's role in the theft of the Sacred Tooth relic, which is Sri Lanka's most prized Buddhist relic. Buddhist texts tell of the arrival of the Buddha's sacred teeth in the 4th century A.D., and the struggles by kings and empires to acquire this relic. The Chinese story of how the Sacred Tooth ended up in China

**D**usk at the Kiri Vihara Temple near Tissamaharana in southern Sri Lanka.

comes to us through an anecdote in the Ming edition of the *Record of the Western Regions in the Tang*. It describes how the relic protected the treasure fleet as it journeyed back to China:

*The elaborate headdress of a traditional Kandyan dancer.*

> *They encountered gigantic waves for hundreds of miles, but these did not disturb the ships for it was as if the fleet were moving across dry land. The fierce dragons beneath the sea and dangerous fish let the ships pass. The men were happy.*

The anecdote goes on to mention that Yongle commanded that an exquisite container encrusted with diamonds and other jewels be made to hold the sacred relic.[7]

Whatever the truth of the mysterious journey of the Sacred Tooth relic to Chinese shores, the venerated object appears safely back in Sinhalese hands during the building of a new shrine to house the relic a few years later. The shrine, of course, was constructed as a three-storey palace for a relic so valuable that it was further encased in four golden bejewelled caskets, each more beautiful and ornate than the next.[8]

Today the Sacred Tooth relic rests in the Sri Dalada Maligawa Temple in Kandy, in central Sri Lanka. A replica of the tooth is venerated during the Dalada Procession, which forms part of the long and complex Kandy Esala Perahera festival each July or August. The two-week long festival features traditional Kandyan dancing and caparisoned elephants.

And what of the trilingual stone tablet that Zheng He brought to Sri Lanka on the third voyage of the treasure fleet? It must have been erected on Sri Lankan soil, for it was discovered in 1911 in the southern port city of Galle, five hundred years after it was brought to Sri Lanka. It is now on permanent display in the National Museum in Colombo.

Watching the fanfare and colour of the Dalada Procession, with its long line of chanting monks, trumpeting elephants, wild drummers, gilded palanquins and dancers decked in silver necklaces and elaborate headdresses, one wonders: did Zheng He and his men ever witness such a spectacle? The modern voyager may ponder that extraordinary period of Sri Lankan and Chinese history, when a eunuch admiral made contact with a Sinhalese hero, as he reads the inscription of Yongle's praise of the Buddha on the stone tablet:

*Deeply do we revere you, merciful and honoured one, whose bright perfection is wide-embracing, and whose way of virtue passes all understanding, whose law pervades all human relations, and the years of whose great era are as numerous as the sands of the river; you whose controlling influence ennobles and converts, whose kindness quickens, and whose strength discerns, whose mysterious efficacy is beyond compare! The mountainous isle of Sri Lanka lies in the south of the ocean, and its Buddhist temples are sanctuaries of your gospel, where your miraculous responsive power imbues and enlightens.*[9]

# What to See and Do in Sri Lanka[10]

## Dalada Maligawa – Temple of the Tooth
**Kandy, Central Sri Lanka in the Cultural Triangle**

One of Buddhism's holiest shrines, this temple houses the famed Sacred Tooth relic of the Buddha mentioned in Chinese records about Sri Lanka during Zheng He's voyages. Don't expect to see the relic, though, for it is safely ensconced behind a diminishing series of caskets and a large outer casket and rarely shown to the public.

The temple and nearby buildings are designated a World Heritage Site and feature a drawbridge, moat and gateway from the 18th century, Buddhist frescoes and excellent wooden carvings in the Kandyan style.

The focus of the temple is of course the worship of the relic, and the best time to visit is during the evening *puja* (ceremony). You will have to contend with the sounds of drums, heavy incense smoke and the crush of crowds for a glimpse of the outer casket. But it's well worth it to get a feel of the intensity and beauty of religious fervour in Sri Lanka.

**A** 17th century map of the Sri Lankan port of Galle when it was under Portuguese rule.

## Historic Fort Town of Galle
**Galle, southern Sri Lanka**

Spend a relaxing day wandering about the old fort town of Galle, a World Heritage Site dating back to the 16th century Portuguese period of Sri Lankan history, and built up by the British in the 19th century. The fort town consists of several hundred buildings that are surrounded by enormous ramparts, the entire structure sitting on a promontory overlooking and surrounded on three sides by the Indian Ocean.

The ramparts are punctuated at intervals by bastions (sections that project outward), which are given poetic names such as Moon, Star Aeolus, Point Utrecht and Neptune. Within the ramparts are colonial buildings with verandahs and arches and historic churches in the Dutch and English styles. An Arab quarter offers a mosque with slender, graceful minarets, and the National Maritime Museum and National Cultural Museum display Sri Lanka's maritime, Dutch and Portuguese heritage.

## Adam's Peak
**Southwestern Sri Lanka**

Chinese descriptions of 15th century Sri Lanka mention this perfectly conical mountain which rises 2,234 metres above sea level as being a great source of rubies and gems. Today, Adam's Peak is a pilgrimage site for Muslims, Buddhists, Hindus and Christians, who all climb the mountain to see a giant "footprint" at the summit. Muslims believe it was left when Adam first came to earth after the Biblical Fall from

The revered Temple of the Tooth, or Sri Dalada Maligawa Temple, in Kandy, central Sri Lanka.

the Garden of Eden. Hindus believe it is the footprint of the god Siva, while Buddhists believe the Buddha was invited by a local king to leave his print on the mountain. Christians maintain the footprint was made by St Thomas, whom they believe came to southern India to spread Christianity in A.D. 50.

The three-to-four-hour climb is fairly easy and usually undertaken during the pilgrimage season between December/ January and mid-April. Start early to reach the top at dawn for spectacular views of the surrounding countryside.

## Yala National Park
### Southeastern Sri Lanka

Yala National Park (sometimes called Ruhuna National Park) is one of Sri Lanka's most well-known nature reserves. Although the Yala Safari Game Lodge was damaged by the December 2004 tsunami, the major part of the park has survived unscathed.

Yala remains a hotspot of biodiversity, with, some say, the highest concentration of elusive leopards in the world. Some 14,000 hectares (34,594 acres) within the park – in the area most easily accessible to visitors – support an astounding 1.1 leopards per square kilometre. Leopards apart, the park is home to macaque and langur monkeys, as well as spotted deer, jackals, wild boars, buffaloes, crocodiles and elephants. Bird life in the park astounds with both land birds such as the Indian Peafowl and Sri Lanka Junglefowl and birds of prey, including the White-bellied Sea Eagle and Painted Stork.

The best time to visit Yala is between October and December, in the early morning or late afternoon.

An ancient rock painting (above) is preserved in central Sri Lanka, at Sigiriya, where the rock formations (below) have been home to monks and royalty for many centuries. Opposite: Ancient ruins at an archaeological site in coastal Sri Lanka.

## Sigiriya
### Central Sri Lanka in the Cultural Triangle

Yet another World Heritage Site, the impregnable fortress of Sigiriya is perched on a rock that rises 182 metres from the plains. The fortress features a royal citadel, water gardens, fountains, a double moat and habitations for ordinary people. King Kasyapa built the complex in A.D. 477, and after his death monks made it their home until the 14th century, when it was abandoned. Archaeologists rediscovered Sigiriya in the 19th century.

The most famous part of the complex is the fresco gallery, with remarkably well-preserved frescoes of apsaras (celestial nymphs) painted red, yellow, green and black. Some of the spirits depicted have Far Eastern and African features, indicating perhaps the cosmopolitan nature of King Kasyapa's court.

The place can get crowded with tourists, so go early in the day for a more peaceful visit.

# The Malabar Coast

*At the end of this great market-festival, Zheng He and the king exchanged gifts of gold and silver, silk and ivory, jewels and porcelain. As the setting sun displayed the most brilliant of its colours, they parted in passionate sorrow. The king and his attendants hold on to*

**A** 19th century print of fisherman off the Malabar coast of Kerala, India.

their treasured silk, porcelain and jewels while Grand Eunuch leads
away the rare animals and birds given to his mission as reciprocal gifts.
Even when they were sailing down the river back to the armada, the
music from instruments made of shells and reeds could still be heard
from land. And the departing visitors knew that their hosts were still on
shore listening to the drums and flutes coming from their boats.

Grand Eunuch Zheng He, the faithful servant of the Ming Emperor,
was sent to the Western Ocean as an imperial emissary to blaze a trail
of glory for the Middle Kingdom. Never did he expect to leave a path of
amazing splendour that would seep into the lives of so many people in
so many places, through so many ways over so long a time...

That evening, Zheng He failed to sleep all night. And his soldiers
and officials softly talked and sang all night long.

— Kuo Pao Kun, *Descendants of the Eunuch Admiral*

**K**ovalam Beach near
Thiruvananthapuram
in Kerala, a popular
destination for tourists.

From Sri Lanka, Zheng He's fleet would visit the Indian coastal
state of Kerala. Like any modern-day voyager riding on the monsoon
winds from Sri Lanka to India, he too would have seen long stretches
of white beaches lined by coconut trees and fishermen going out
to sea in large rowing boats. Kerala was the final destination for
the earlier voyages of the fleet, and the base from which the later
expeditions explored Arabian and African shores.

*Though the journey from this country to the Middle Kingdom is
more than a hundred thousand li, yet the people are very similar, happy,
and prosperous, with identical customs. We have here engraved a
stone, a perpetual declaration for ten thousand ages.*[11]

This is the inscription on a stone erected by men of the treasure fleet in the city of Calicut, named Kozhikode in present-day Kerala, India, during the inauguration of a new king, Mana Vikraman. The event took place with Chinese blessings during Zheng He's second expedition from China in 1407.

The Chinese knew Calicut, at the other end of China's sea routes to the West, as the "great country of the Western Ocean".[12] Guli, as the Chinese called Calicut, was a trading hub in the 15th century. Together with Quilon and Cochin, two other city-states on the Malabar coast, it made up the famed Spice Coast of Kerala. Here, in the cool hinterlands, grow acres of pepper plants and other fabulous spices such as cardamom, cinnamon and turmeric. The Western Ghats, a mountain range in the east of the state, is a good source of hardwoods such as teak and mahogany, as well as scented sandalwood and rosewood.

Such access to great natural wealth was a source of power and drew many to the Spice Coast. It was an important stop not only for Zheng He's treasure fleet, but also for traders and seafarers from all across the Indian Ocean.

Today's bustling ports of Cochin, Calicut and Quilon would probably still be recognisable to the men of Zheng He's fleet. Chinese fishing nets, said to have been introduced to the Malabar coast in the Yuan dynasty (A.D. 1271–1368), can be found strung along the beaches in Cochin, Quilon and other parts of the coast. These huge ladle-like scoops supported by weights and counterweights are a visual reminder of the early links between Kerala and China.

Ma Huan, one of many Chinese Muslim interpreters who sailed with Zheng He, described the people of Kerala as trustworthy and honest with an appearance that was "smart, fine and distinguished".[13] Visitors to the state today may recognise some of these traits in Keralites, with their typically codified and conservative hierarchies and behaviour. Kerala culture is highly literate and artistic. Ma Huan is said to have been amazed at the ability of traders to work out quite accurately the complicated mathematics of bartering using the digits of fingers and toes,[14] a practice that the older Keralites still remember being taught in school.

**Two 17th century maps portray the Kerala towns of Cannanore (top) and Cochin (bottom). Opposite: A devotee lights lamps in a Sri Lankan temple.**

## "In such and such a moon…"

Ma Huan gives a lively description of how trade was conducted in Calicut when the treasure fleet arrived in port. Zheng He's representative would first meet with an Indian middleman to set a date to discuss the prices of goods for barter. On that day, both men would look at everything on the ships that was available for trade

**S**yrian Christians in Kottayam, central Kerala, celebrate Saint George's Day with a procession of relics.

and decide a price for each item. Having done so, they would recite special words to seal the prices:

*"In such and such a moon, on such and such a day, we have all joined hands and sealed our agreement with a hand-clap; whether [the price] is dear or cheap, we will never repudiate it or change it."*[15]

The same practice was applied to the Indian goods on offer, whether pepper or precious stones. According to Ma Huan, the process could take up to three months. At the Pepper Exchange in Cochin today, similar haggling takes place, with telephones ringing away and brokers yelling out prices and amounts in Malayalam.

Ma Huan also recorded some of the customs and legends of the people of Kerala. Interestingly, a story handed down to us by Ma Huan resembles quite closely the story of Moses and the Golden Calf. In Ma Huan's account, Mouxie was a holy man who "established a religious cult". Later, Mouxie went away and placed his brother in charge. His brother, however, "began to have depraved ideas". He fashioned a golden calf and "taught the people to listen to his bidding and to adore the gold ox, saying 'It always excretes gold.'"[16] Quite possibly, Ma Huan met the Jews of Cochin, where a Jewish settlement survives to this day, in severely reduced numbers.

Kerala's complex religious make-up – there are Hindus, Muslims, Syrian Christians and Jews – was also no doubt instrumental in the Chinese notion that India was the origin of all the world's great religions known to them in the 15th century. An unofficial history of the period, the *Ming tong jian*, tells us that India was divided into five parts, that from central India came Buddhism, and that western India gave rise to both Christianity and Islam. The record goes on to note that one of the discoveries Zheng He made on his trips to India was that the land of the Arabs (Tian Fang), the birthplace of Islam, was much more to the southwest of India.[17]

Today, take a walk in any of Kerala's towns and you'll see churches, mosques and temples, all thronging with people performing centuries-old traditions and customs, very much as Zheng He and his men would have witnessed on their trips to the Malabar coast.

Chinese political influence along the Malabar coast was strong during the time of Zheng He's voyages. Not only were Keralite emissaries being transported to and from the Ming capital in China on these mega-ships, but some of the zamorins, traditional rulers of the city-states of Malabar, were also appointed by Chinese decree. A tablet for the zamorin of Cochin tells of how all nations everywhere follow the law of the emperor, that "when our imperial orders arrived, [Cochin's] officials received them with their arms raised and their knees bent midst pounding drums". The tablet goes on to say that "the teachings of the sages of China have benefited [Cochin]…", that "violent winds have not arisen, torrential rains have not fallen, pestilence and plagues have ceased, and there have been no disasters and calamities".[18] All a result, the tablet says, of Cochin having adopted the "kingly culture" of Imperial China.

If somewhat over the top in describing Kerala as being given the "gift" of Chinese civilisation, the tablet nevertheless records a unique relationship between this balmy, sun and surf-drenched part of India, with its rich natural and cultural wealth, on the one hand, and a truly outward-looking Ming China on the other.

# What to See and Do in Kerala[19]

## Thiruvananthapuram (Trivandrum)
**Southern Kerala**

Thiruvananthapuram, or Trivandrum as it used to be called, is the state capital of Kerala. It takes its name from Anantha, the serpent who is the mount of the city deity Padmanabha. The mythic origins of the city can be enjoyed at the Sri Padmanabhaswamy Temple, just off the Chalai Bazaar Road. Here the city deity and his serpent are represented by a six-metre figure divided into three sections.

The main hall of the temple features some 360 granite pillars, while the inner sanctum is reached by means of a 130 metre colonnade that is 8 metres wide. Non-Hindus are not normally permitted to visit the temple, but exceptions may be made for those wearing traditional Indian clothing – a sari for women and a dhoti for men. Festivals are an excellent time to see the temple come alive with processions, music, drumming and dancing.

The main festival periods are March/April and October/November, when temple idols are transported with great ceremony and accompanied by members of Kerala's ancient royal family, the Maharajahs of Travancore, to the Lakshadweep Sea for ritual bathing.

# Jewtown, Kochi (Cochin)
## Central Kerala, along the coast

There is a synagogue in Jewtown, Cochin, whose foundation dates to 1568. It is not the oldest synagogue in Kerala however; there is at least one other that dates to 1344. Hand-painted tiles brought from Guangdong in the 18th century can be seen in the Jewtown synagogue. The synagogue is open from Sunday to Friday, from 10 a.m. until noon, and again from 3 p.m. to 5 p.m.

Jewtown is also the home of Cochin's spice trade and antiques trade. The Pepper Exchange, where spices are traded, is open Monday to Friday from 10 a.m. to 1 p.m. and from 2 p.m. to 4 p.m. On Saturdays it is open to the public from 10 a.m. to 12.30 p.m.

# The Backwaters
## Coastline from Kollam (Quilon) to Allapuzha

The backwaters of Kerala is a unique environment forged by the action of the sea and tides. It consists of ponds, canals, lagoons, rivers and lakes that run several kilometres inland from the sea. This water-based lifestyle has been the backbone of the local economy for centuries, with whole villages lining water bodies of various sizes that support fishing, prawn farming, animal rearing and agriculture, particularly coconut plantations.

Kerala's multi-religious mix can also be seen in the Jewish synagogue (opposite) that still serves a very small Jewish community. Below: A boat trip along the backwaters is a highlight of any trip to Kerala.

Rent a boat for the 8-hour journey between Kollam and Allapuzha to see Kerala life unwind at a leisurely pace. There are stops at temples and villages to witness dance performances, boat-building and coir making.

## Periyar Wildlife Sanctuary
### Western Ghats, Eastern Kerala

The Periyar Wildlife Sanctuary is almost 800 square kilometres of highlands in eastern Kerala. The park's flora includes evergreen and deciduous forests and grasslands, while faunal life includes elephants, tigers, bison, wild boars and antelopes. Spotting wildlife is rare, however, and most visitors are content to tour the sanctuary via a spin on the 26 square kilometre artificial lake. Trekking tours can be arranged and there are numerous options for accommodation both inside and outside the reserve. You have a better chance of seeing wildlife if you pass a night in one of the observation towers or resthouses located deep within the sanctuary. These provide basic shelter, so bring your own food and bedding.

# Kathakali Dance

In Kathakali, one of Kerala's best-known dance forms, the exponents don elaborate costumes and make-up for performances that can last many hours. Themes of the dance drama are taken from the stories of the Hindu epics *Mahabharata* and *Ramayana*. Larger-than-life heroes and villains narrate the story through complicated facial gestures, hand actions and eye movements, while singers chant the texts using a Sanskritised version of Malayalam, the language of Kerala.

The modern version of the art form has been considerably shortened to keep young people interested, but the Ernakulam Kathakali Club just outside of Cochin puts on traditional all-night performances once a month, while the See India Foundation, also in Ernakulam, prefaces the performances with a lecture in English on the history and elements of Kathakali. Arrive early for performances and you will be rewarded by the sight of performers transforming themselves into their dance characters.

**M**asked dancers perform a traditional Kathakali dance, one of Kerala's many highly stylised dance forms.

# Zheng He's Voyages to the Middle East

Zheng He's fleet reached Hormuz in the Middle East on the fourth voyage, which left China in January 1414. On the fifth voyage, the fleet stopped at Hormuz and Aden. The sixth voyage also saw the fleet visiting Aden. The seventh and final voyage of the treasure ships that departed Chinese shores in 1432 brought them to Hormuz, Aden, Jeddah and Dhofar.

**M**ap of the Middle East produced in 1570 by Dutch mapmaker Abraham Ortelius for his *Atlas Theatrum Orbis Terrarum* (*Theatre of the World*).

In almost 30 years, Zheng He and his imperial armada visited Campa, Panduranga, Cape Varella, Pulo Condore, Gelam Island, Siam, Palembang, Malacca, Pulo Sembilan, Sumudra, Battak, Lengkasuka, Bras Island, Nicobar Islands, Silan, Quilon, Cochin, Calicut, Ormuz, al-Ahsa, Bangala, Camboja, Pulo Aor, Tamiang, Governador Strait (Longyamen), Langkawi, Gili Timor, Pahang, Mindoro, Karimata, Jangala, Surabaya, Brunei, Solot, Aden, Zufar, Jobo, Mogadishu, Maldives Islands, Brawa, Mecca, Harwa Aru, Litai, Lambri....

For almost 30 years, Zheng He ploughed the South China Sea and the Indian Ocean. He wandered the wilderness at sea and on land, tens of thousands of miles away from his home, his nation, his emperor and lord. An outcast almost for life, exiled on the vast, open sea, he – apart from serving the emperor's imperial interest – also must have been looking, deep in his heart, for his own paradise.

— Kuo Pao Kun, Descendants of the Eunuch Admiral

Muslim pilgrims during the *haj* to Mecca touch the base of the Multazam, which is the only door of the Ka'bah, the large stone building that is the holiest shrine in Islam. The hanging embroidered with gold and silver Arabic calligraphy in front of the door is part of the *kiswa*, a silk cloth that covers the stone Ka'bah. It is believed that members of Zheng He's fleet may have performed the *haj* pilgrimage while the ships docked at Jeddah on the seventh voyage from China, between 1431 and 1433.

# To the Persian Gulf and Arabia Felix

The year is 1417, and it has been 12 years since the launch of the great treasure fleet. The Yongle emperor, setting his sights on the Middle East, has just issued orders that Zheng He take the fleet beyond the familiar sea routes to India. Perhaps in ordering the admiral to Hormuz in the Persian Gulf, Yongle was eager to learn what lay beyond South Asia.

During those 12 years, much of the coastal regions of South and Southeast Asia had already experienced the immense wealth and scale of the Chinese treasure fleet, with its huge ships, thousands of soldiers and tons of precious cargo.

The fleet had anchored in the ports of Cochin, Quilon, Calicut and Galle, and those on board would no doubt have heard of places like Aden, Hormuz and Mombasa on the African coast. They would also have seen precious goods such as frankincense from Dhofar in Oman, and ivory from East Africa in the port markets of India and Sri Lanka.

Some scholars are inclined to view the fifth and later voyages of the treasure fleet as having the primary purpose of discovery; in other words, seeking distant rulers who could fall into the tribute system came second to discovery. Others see the new impetus to the voyages as "a very personal expression of the ambition and megalomania of the third Ming emperor and, as such, a unique expression in Chinese history."[1]

Traditional Egyptian *felouk* (opposite) sail down the Nile at Aswan, Egypt and (above) lie moored on the bank with their characteristic single triangular sail rolled up. Although Zheng He's fleet is not known to have visited Egypt proper, they did make stops in territory in Saudi Arabia ruled by Egyptian caliphs.

In 1416, Yongle had declared that the "seas had been conquered and there was quiet in the four corners".[2] Perhaps this very "quiet" caused Yongle to become restless to see just how far the treasure fleet could travel. Whatever his motivation, the voyages from 1417 onwards would bring Chinese influence to the western Indian Ocean. They would call to mind the epithet that the Ming voyages had turned the vast Indian Ocean into an easily navigable Chinese lake.

# The Island of Hormuz

Hormuz was first visited on the fourth voyage of the treasure fleet, which left China's shores in January 1414. For this voyage, Zheng He had hired the Arabic translator Ma Huan of Hangzhou. Ma Huan's *Ying yai sheng lan* (*Overall Survey of the Ocean Shores*), completed in the mid-1430s and published in 1451, remains one of the very few surviving records written by men who travelled with Zheng He.

Hormuz island lies off the southern coast of Iran (to which it belongs today), right at the entrance to the Persian Gulf. In the 14th century Hormuz was the centre of a very lucrative trade in luxury products from countries surrounding the Gulf. Pearls from Bahrain further north, frankincense from the Musandam Peninsula at the tip of Arabia, silver jewellery from Oman – all flowed into the heaving bazaars of Hormuz to be traded for Chinese silks, Indian cotton and African ivory. Gold, copper, iron, cinnabar and all sorts of precious gems such as rubies and sapphires were to be found in Hormuz.[3]

Ma Huan described the people of Hormuz as wealthy, and "handsome, distinctive and elegant" in their style of dress. He also noted their civic-mindedness; "if a family meets with misfortune resulting in poverty, everyone gives them clothes and food and capital, and relieves their distress," he wrote. Consequently, poverty was at a minimum.[4]

**A** 19th century print depicts the Arabian coastline and an imposing fort.

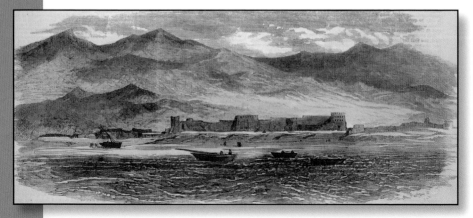

Hormuz today, a rocky outcrop with very little on it, bears no resemblance to the island at its zenith in Zheng He's time. The main trade routes shifted to the Iranian mainland during the 16th century, when the island was occupied by the Portuguese, and that spelt the end of Hormuz's control of the Persian Gulf trade.

The site of the Portuguese fort is worth visiting, but nothing is left from the time of the treasure fleet. The museums of Teheran do, however, hold substantial collections of Chinese porcelain and other trade goods from different periods of Chinese history, as the Silk Road passed close to the Iranian plateau on the way to the Mediterranean.

# Exotic Aden[5]

The treasure fleet visited Aden for the first time during their fifth voyage. Aden, on the southern coast of the Arabian Peninsula in present-day Yemen, lay smack in the middle of sea routes between India and the African coast. The wealth of ancient Yemen came from the trade in frankincense that traversed the shores of southern Arabia. The legendary Queen of Sheba, who tested the wisdom of King Solomon, is said by some to have lived here, lending Yemen an air of adventure and romance.

Sailing into Aden's port, Zheng He and his treasure fleet would have been greeted by a wild and craggy coastline dominated by dark volcanic rock. A 20th century traveller describes the scene thus:

*The rocks of Aden stand up like dolomites, so jagged and old...*
*There is a feeling of gigantic naked force about it all, and one thinks*

**H**ouses built in
traditional Yemeni
style cling to the rocks
in this village in Yemen.

*what it was when these hills were boiling out their stream of fire,
hissing them out into the sea, and wonders at anything so fragile as
man living on these ancient desolations.*[6]

Ma Huan's chronicles give us a wealth of information about
Aden and its people. Its military influence was strong, and the city
was protected by several thousand "well-drilled horsemen and foot
soldiers". Aden's wealth, he wrote, could be seen from its women,
who covered themselves in jewellery of gold and precious stones.

Zheng He's fleet was ceremoniously received by the sultan
of Aden, who encouraged precious goods to be traded with the
Chinese. He also offered some pretty amazing tribute gifts to the
Yongle emperor in the form of exotic animals such as leopards, a
giraffe and ostriches, as well as a plaque engraved with gold leaf.
Zheng He personally received golden belts and hats studded with
precious stones.[7]

# What to See and Do in Yemen

High in the lush highlands of Yemen's interior, spectacular Sana'a, the
capital of modern Yemen, still transports visitors to medieval Arabia
with its veiled women, bustling souks, tribal warriors in *abas*, and
classical inns called *funduqs*.

Yemeni architecture in Sana'a is probably the most fascinating and unique in all of the Arab world. The city sprouts sleek citadels from craggy outcrops, the styles of which hark back to Old Sumeria and Babylon. The different floors of houses are marked on the outside of the towers with decorative reliefs, and windows and doors are similarly ornamented with arches and coloured glass. Whitewashed, the whole composition is quite stunning, especially at sunrise and sundown, when the whole city positively glows.

Walking in the old part of Sana'a is the best way to appreciate not only the architecture of the city, but also its street life and colourful souks. The spice souk and the silver souk are very popular with tourists, the former for the piles and piles of freshly ground pepper, cumin, coriander and cloves, and the latter for the intricate silver jewellery executed by Jewish silversmiths.

Outside Sana'a, stunning palaces perch on a steep outcrop. The summer palace of Imam Yahya at Wadi Dhar is built in traditional Yemeni style although it only dates from the 1930s.

**T**raditional Yemeni daggers, their handles fashioned from rhinoceros horn.

**B**arrel-loads of tomatoes, onions and potatoes line the market in Sana'a, the capital city of Yemen.

Aden, the Yemeni port that Zheng He's treasure fleet visited, is not as busy today as it used to be. As late as the 19th century, when British colonial influence was at its peak, Aden was the most important coaling station and transshipment stop between India and England. It became the third largest port in the world (after New York and London) when the Suez Canal opened in 1869.

Colonial influences remain in Aden today in the form of British-style hotels in the Tawahi district. The old harbour of Aden, where the treasure fleet would probably have docked, lies in the Crater district, Aden's oldest and most Arab quarter, with its traditional oriental souk.

# The Treasure Fleet in Dhofar and Jeddah

On the seventh and last voyage of the treasure fleet, which left China's shores in 1432 bound for East Africa, the fleet also stopped at Dhofar in present-day Oman, at the southern tip of the Saudi peninsula, and at Jeddah on the Red Sea, the main port of modern Saudi Arabia.[8]

The Chinese were very interested in Arab medicines and herbs. In Jeddah they obtained aloe, myrrh, benzoin, storax and mormodica seeds, which could be used to treat a host of symptoms, from ulcers, wounds and inflammations to poor circulation and respiratory illnesses.[9] Another precious cargo was frankincense, the best of which could be found in Dhofar.

Because it is the only part of the Saudi peninsula to receive the southwest monsoon (the same monsoon that drove the treasure fleet across the Indian Ocean and the South China Sea back to China), Dhofar is lush with oases and waterfalls. Frankincense trees grow in the hills and mountains set away from the coast. The trees grow to about 5 metres high and have large gnarled branches extending from the base of the trunk. Frankincense is the white gum resin of the tree after it dries and turns crystalline. When burned, these crystals give off the aromatic scent that so enthralled the ancient world.

Ma Huan has left us a description of Mecca and Medina, the holiest cities of Islam today situated in Saudi Arabia. His accounts, however, are not particularly accurate and perhaps obtained second-hand from traders in Jeddah who may have made the trip.

**M**ecca during the *haj* pilgrimage hosts hundreds of thousands of devout Muslims. Although Ma Huan claims to have visited Mecca in his writings, some scholars are not inclined to think so. Overleaf: The elegant interior of a mosque in Jeddah, Saudi Arabia.

# Zheng He's Voyages to Africa

Zheng He's fleet reached Africa's shores during the fifth voyage that sailed from China in 1417. The ships were returning ambassadors from Mogadishu and Brawa in Somalia and Mombasa and Malindi in Kenya. The sixth voyage saw the fleet stopping again at Mogadishu and Swahili towns further south along the coast. The seventh and final voyage of the treasure fleet also called on East African ports as far south as Malindi in Kenya.

The African portion of Abraham Ortelius's *Theatrum Orbis Terrarum*, or *Theatre of the World*, published in 1570. This work is considered the first modern atlas, with its uniform map sheets and book binding.

With divine command from the Ming Emperor in 1405
He brought the imperial influence to distant nations

Over the treacherous straits and thunderous seas
He braved savage waters to explore the Western lands

For three decades Zheng He's armada ruled the ocean
Exploring the exotic from Tenggara, India to Arabia

When he returned to the splendours of the Imperial Court
Peace and friendship had stretched as far as Africa

— Kuo Pao Kun, Descendants of the Eunuch Admiral

**W**ildebeest graze on the savanna plains of the Maasai Mara in Kenya. Zheng He's fleet brought back many East African animals to China, among them various types of antelope, giraffes and ostriches.

# To Africa's Swahili Coast

**Z**heng He's voyages eventually stretched as far as the Swahili coast of East Africa, a land that amazed the Chinese. An account of the reception of African envoys and their animals at the Ming court of Yongle in 1419 describes the sheer wonder and awe that accompanied their visit. The Chinese audience "craning their necks looked on with pleasure, and stamping their feet when they were scared and startled, thinking that these were things that were rarely heard of in the world and that China had never seen their likeness"[1] East Africa astounds even modern visitors with its natural beauty and rich culture.

The Swahili culture that Zheng He's treasure fleet would have observed in East Africa evolved from Islamic, African and Asian influences. In fact, the very word *Swahili* is derived from the Arab for "coast", *sahil*. (Swahili, the language of much of East Africa, is one of Africa's most extensively spoken languages.)

A maritime culture centred on the sea, Swahili culture has developed distinctive styles in music, architecture, literature and customs. Add to this culture the incredible flora and fauna that one sees during a typical East African safari (*safari* is Swahili for "journey"), and visitors are assured a holiday filled with sights not seen anywhere else on the planet.

**W**eatherbeaten boats moor in the shallow waters off Lamu Island on the East African coast. Above: An old print of an Arab vessel being pursued by a European ship (in the background).

# African "Qilin"

One of the most famous tribute gifts to China were giraffes from East Africa. The first giraffe arrived in the Chinese court in 1414, a gift from the newly crowned king of Bengal, Saifu'd-Din, who had been given the giraffe by the king of Malindi (now a town in Kenya).

The Chinese had never quite seen anything like them: tall creatures with endless legs and necks, short horns, a long tongue and gentle eyes framed by long lashes. To the astonished court, these animals were *qilin*, beasts of the literary imagination appearing only when the world was at harmony and the emperor virtuous. Many no doubt thought the gift indicated not only the wisdom of their emperor, but also that the world was united under China's benevolent civilising power. With due fanfare, a painting of the animal was commissioned and a hymn of praise to Yongle and his family composed:[2]

*In a corner of the western seas, in the stagnant*
*    waters of a great morass,*
*Truly was produced a qilin, whose shape was*
*    as high as fifteen feet,*
*With the body of a deer and the tail of an ox,*
*    and a fleshy, boneless horn,*
*With luminous spots like a red cloud or purple mist.*
*Its hoofs do not tread on [living] beings and in its wanderings it*
*    carefully selects its ground,*
*It walks in stately fashion and in its every*
*    motion it observes a rhythm,*
*Its harmonious voice sounds like a bell or a*
*    musical tube.*

Zebras and giraffes were also received as tribute gifts from African rulers during the time of the voyages of the treasure fleet.

*Gentle is this animal, that in all antiquity has*
    *been seen but once,*
*The manifestation of its divine spirit rises up to heaven's abode.*[3]

Two years later, Yongle journeyed to the palace gates in Nanjing to receive yet more amazing animals from Malindi, including what were described as "celestial horses" and "celestial stags" (probably species of antelope and zebra) – and another "qilin". He is quoted as saying "This event is due to the abundant virtue of the late emperor, my father, and also to the assistance rendered me by my ministers. That is why distant people arrive in uninterrupted succession."[4]

The giraffe continued to play a small but symbolic role in the voyages of the treasure fleet, with several arriving at court during the time of Zheng He's voyages.[5] Almost 600 years later, it again took centre stage when the Chinese prime minister visited Kenya in 1983 and China's *People's Daily* wrote about the role of the animal in Sino-African relations.[6] In 1988, two giraffes were presented to China on the occasion of the Kenyan president's visit to China.

**A** Chinese painting from the Ming period records the gift of a giraffe to the Ming emperor.

# Early Contact with Africa

China's knowledge of Africa stretches to several hundred years before Zheng He's voyages, which in itself is remarkable. How this knowledge was gained is not clear. Was it as a result of actual visits to the region, or from Arab, Indian and Persian traders who had known Africa? Chinese 12th century records speak of an island in the ocean that supplied slaves, that some have suggested is Madagascar, a large island off the coast of Mozambique in southern Africa.

*[In the west] there is an island in the sea on which there are many savages. Their bodies are as black as lacquer and they have frizzled hair. They are enticed by [offers of] food and then captured and sold as slaves to Arabic countries, where they fetch a very high price. They are employed as gatekeepers, and it is said that they have no longing for their kinfolk.*[7]

An even earlier record, from the 9th century, describes the East African custom of extracting blood from the jugular vein of a cow, a practice of the Maasai, arguably Africa's most famous tribal group, who live not far from Kenya's Indian Ocean coastline. Nomadic herdsmen of the Oromo, Dar, Dir and other groups that live in various parts of Northeast and East Africa also follow this practice.[8]

*The country of Bobali [thought to be Berbera in Somalia] is in the southwestern ocean. [The people] do not eat any of the five grains*

*but eat only meat. They often stick a needle into the veins of cattle and draw blood, which they drink raw, mixed with milk. They wear no clothes except that they cover [the parts] below the loins with sheepskins. Their women are clean and of proper behaviour. The inhabitants themselves kidnap them and sell them to strangers at prices many times more than they would fetch at home. The country produces ivory and ambergris.*[9]

It is interesting that these records mention slavery, which was widespread in the ancient world, whether in China or East Africa. Slavery on the African coast had been an accepted economic activity for many centuries. It is believed the practice began as a way of repaying a debt. A child would be "loaned" to a rich relative in return for food or other goods and the child would then work off the debt. Usually, however, such persons remained slaves throughout their lives. Later, the more direct practice developed, with African traders rounding up tribal peoples from the hinterland and selling them off to Arab or other foreign traders who visited the Swahili coast.

Descriptions of African slaves in China include a 12th century account of wealthy Chinese who kept African slaves as gatekeepers and Africans employed to swim under ships to fix leaks in the hull because of a belief that they swam without blinking![10]

Other Chinese sources mention names of places along the East African coast, including Bibaluo, Zengba and Zengbaluo. Like Bobali, Bibaluo is thought to be Berbera on the Somali coast, while Zengba and Zengbaluo could be a phonetic rendition of the Arab Zangibar. A 13th century record of Bibaluo tells us that the country produced elephant tusks and rhinoceros horns.[11] The people of a country called Zhongli, also believed to be on the East African coast, are described as going "with heads uncovered and barefoot":

> They wrap a cloth round themselves but do not dare wear jackets: only the chief ministers and the king's entourage wear jackets and wrap turbans round their heads as a mark of distinction. The king's residence is made of bricks and slabs of stone, the people's houses of palm fronds and thatch roofing.[12]

This information comes to us from Zhao Rugua, who lived in the early 13th century, two hundred years before Zheng He's time. A customs inspector, Zhao made it a point to gather information from traders transiting at his port of Quanzhou. His description of the strict class distinctions and stone buildings in Zhongli could refer to the Shirazi who settled on the East African coast from the late 12th century onwards and claimed descent from Shiraz in Persia. A powerful political group, they gained control of many of the ports. Indeed, Swahili culture evolved as a result of the mixing of Islamic Shirazi culture and indigenous African customs. The Shirazi also built stone settlements, ruins of which can be seen in Kenya and Tanzania. The most famous Shirazi town is Zanzibar off the coast of Tanzania. Zhao gives more details of Zhongli's inhabitants:

> Many people practise magical arts, and can change themselves into birds, beasts or sea-creatures, to frighten and delude the foolish commoners. If in their business dealings with a foreign ship a grievance arises, they cast a spell to bring the ship to a standstill, so that it cannot move forwards or backwards; and only when the crew has consented to make peace will they let them go.[13]

Traditional Arab dhows off the coast of Kenya. These boats are still used by fishermen.

This account may sound unbelievable, yet it is known that the Shirazi elite used the threat of witchcraft and other magical arts to control their people. And the story of bringing ships to a standstill was one that was common in parts of southern Somalia.[14]

# The Treasure Fleet on the Swahili Coast

Mogadishu and Brawa in Somalia were two of the treasure fleet's ports of call in East Africa during its fifth voyage. The fleet left China in 1417 to return ambassadors from these cities. Zheng He's fleet had taken these emissaries on board in either Calicut or Hormuz on the previous voyage and had transported them to China.

On the sixth voyage of the treasure fleet, which also called at ports along the Swahili coast, Fei Xin, one of Zheng He's officers, describes Mogadishu as being "intolerably hot". He adds that "since there is no cultivated soil, [the people] live on fishing. Because of the torrid weather only a few plants can grow… [and] if anyone wandered over this country he would have only met with sad glances". For Fei Xin, Somalia was "an entire land having nothing but sand", and this is an accurate description of southern Somalia.[15]

A novel, the 16th century *Journey of the three-jewelled eunuch to the Western Oceans*, states that the treasure ships were involved in military action against a walled town called La-sa, believed to be close to Mogadishu, and that the ruler of Mogadishu was suspicious of the Chinese ships, saying "the Ming empire and our country are thousands of miles apart, and today without reason it has sent soldiers against us. Obviously, they want to take us over."[16] Whether fighting ever took place is disputed, even though the novel is supposedly based on an account by Gong Zhen,[17] another of Zheng He's officers, and the official history of the Ming dynasty.

# What to See and Do in East Africa

## Cradle of Mankind

East Africa is known as the "Cradle of Mankind" because it is believed that human beings as we know them today first evolved in this arid place. The region is home to some of the oldest human bones ever discovered. Some of the most spectacular finds have been made in Ethiopia (the skeleton of a female discovered in 1974, believed to be more than three million years old, and nicknamed Lucy) and Tanzania. Olduvai Gorge in Tanzania's Ngorongoro Conservation Area is the site of the fossil discoveries that date to about two million years before the present era. Footprints of humanlike beings that walked upright found in 1979 at nearby Laetoli date to between 3.6 and 3.8 million years before the present era. Fossils of over 30 humans have been identified in the gorge.

Olduvai is also rich in animal fossils, with bones belonging to some 150 mammal species already identified. Among them are those of the deinotherium, a huge elephant-like mammal, and the hipparion, an animal with three hooves resembling a horse. A museum at Olduvai Gorge documents all these finds and explains what life was like all those millions of years ago.

## Serengeti National Park and Maasai Mara Game Reserve

Two of the most famous wildlife parks in the world are Tanzania's Serengeti National Park and Kenya's Maasai Mara. They straddle the Kenya-Tanzania border and animals are free to wander between both nature reserves, which results in some of the most amazing animal migrations ever witnessed on earth.

The annual wildebeest migration sees thousands and thousands of wildebeest and other animals moving in great herds across the massive expanse of East African savanna. Sometimes the herds split, then rejoin. They cross wide rivers and many perish. The wildebeest move in a northerly direction from Serengeti toward Maasai Mara in search of pasture in the dry season at the end of June. They return to Serengeti in November, at the start of the wet season.

These national parks also teem with giraffes, elephants, lions, cheetahs, a large variety of antelope, and an even larger variety of birds and smaller wildlife. The giraffes that sailed halfway round the

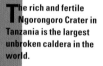

**The rich and fertile Ngorongoro Crater in Tanzania is the largest unbroken caldera in the world.**

world to China from East Africa as gifts for the Ming emperor were probably caught in this part of East Africa.

## African Chinoiserie

The Chinese favoured African products for many reasons: ivory for palanquins and belt clasps; rhinoceros horn as an aphrodisiac and for carvings; tortoiseshell made into a gum to treat consumption; frankincense as a tonic to aid circulation; ambergris (a waxy substance secreted by whales) as a tonic, a lamp fuel, and to perfume the air.[18]

Africans, on the other hand, were much enamoured of Chinese porcelain, which has been discovered across the eastern coast of Africa, from halfway down the Red Sea to the southern tip of Madagascar. Along the East African coast, Chinese porcelain decorate mosques, roofs, walls, doorways and particularly tombs shaped like pillars. Many of these finds are in East African museums, and some are at archaeological sites, including Mambrui near Malindi in Kenya, Kunduchi near Dar-es-Salaam in Tanzania, and at the mausoleum in Siyu on Pate Island. They point to quite a lively stream of trading activities between regions thousands of miles apart.[19]

## Pate Island

Pate Island in the Lamu Archipelago off the coast of northern Kenya has been the site of some speculation by writers and scholars interested in travels of Zheng He's treasure fleet. Louise Levathes, in her book *When China Ruled the Seas*,[20] points to a number of things suggesting that the island could have had a thriving Chinese community during the time of the treasure fleet. Fishermen here

apparently have a lighter skin tone than other Swahili fishermen, and certain members of the Washanga tribe claim descent from shipwrecked Chinese sailors. Craftsmen in the town of Siyu carve intricate designs on lacquered doors in a way more similar to Chinese than Swahili methods, and a small lion carved in the Chinese style was unearthed, its metal content similar to Song dynasty coins.

Pate also had a thriving silk industry when the Portuguese appeared on the East African coast in the 16th century. According to a Portuguese Jesuit, Pate had "very rich silk cloths, from which the Portuguese derive great profit in other Moorish cities where they are not to be had, because they are only manufactured on Pate, and are sent to the others from that place".[21] Could Pate's ancient silk industry have had its origins in a Chinese community on the island?

Whatever the case may be, Pate is worth a visit for its historic stone town of Siyu, which dates from the 15th century, and the Shanga ruins, parts of which go back to the 8th and 9th centuries. You can find tombs here decorated with porcelain.

Neighbouring Lamu Island has a beautiful old stone town that features winding alleys and traditional Swahili architecture.

## Mombasa

Mombasa is the oldest city in Kenya and the largest coastal city both in Kenya and on the East African coast. A cosmopolitan mix of people of Swahili, African, Arab, Indian, Pakistani, Chinese and Caucasian backgrounds makes the city a fascinating place to experience age-old customs and traditions.

The most visited tourist attraction in Mombasa is Fort Jesus, the 16th century Portuguese fort that sits at the harbour entrance. A museum within displays ceramics and trading goods of historic significance to this part of the coast, as well as artefacts from a Portuguese frigate that sank off the coast in the late 17th century.

**M**ombasa beaches are some of the most beautiful around the Indian Ocean.

It's worthwhile to explore Mombasa's old town, which is full of narrow alleyways and houses built in the traditional Swahili style, with overhanging balconies and intricately carved doors and windows.

Mombasa also has beautiful mosques, many situated in the old town and some dating from the 16th century. They are not generally open to non-Muslims, but well worth a walk-by as many of the fine architectural elements such as doors, domes and minarets can be viewed from outside. Some of the more well-known mosques include Mandhry Mosque, Burhani Bohra Mosque, and the Jamat-Khana Mosque.

Both Mombasa and the town of Malindi to the north sent emissaries to Yongle's court in China, and they travelled there on Zheng He's ships. Note the amount of Chinese ceramics plastered into many old East African Islamic tombs as decoration.

## Zanzibar Stone Town

One of the highlights of Tanzania's coast is old Stone Town on Zanzibar Island, another maze of long and narrow alleyways covered by overhanging balconies.

The oldest building on the island is the early 12th century mosque at Kizimkazi at the island's southern tip, while most of Stone Town's buildings date from the 18th and 19th centuries. The old fort, built in 1700, now houses the Zanzibari Cultural Centre, where performances of traditional Zanzibari music are held. Close to the fort is the Beit el-Ajaib, or House of Wonders, Zanzibar's tallest building. It was the first building on the island to have electricity, a "wonder" when it was built in 1883 and hence its name. The ornate wooden carvings here are typical of Zanzibari style.

Just beyond the fort and overlooking the ocean are the Jamituri Gardens, which operates numerous stalls selling delicious foods and grills. Visit the central market to experience bustling and noisy crowds and wander the isles stacked with colourful and aromatic spices and fresh produce.

Walking is by far the easiest way to see the Stone Town's wonderful mix of traditional Zanzibari architecture and other styles, including English, Portuguese and modern style.

## Mount Kilimanjaro and Mount Kenya

Mount Kilimanjaro in Tanzania and Mount Kenya in Kenya are the two most important peaks in East Africa. Kilimanjaro, at 5,895 metres above sea level, is Africa's highest peak and the largest free-standing mountain in the world. It is also one of the world's tallest dormant

**Fruits for sale at the market of Zanzibar's Stone Town.**

volcanoes. Ernest Hemingway described the mountain thus: "as wide as all the world, great, high, and unbelievably white in the sun, was the square top of Kilimanjaro."

Lush rainforest covers the lower slopes. As you ascend, you pass scrublands, then alpine moorlands, before reaching the ice fields. The summit is often covered by clouds during the day, so it is worth rising very early to see the view in the morning. The climb is easy, however, for the reasonably fit. Just be sure to give yourself sufficient time to get acclimatised to the altitude. Scientists believe that the snow-capped peaks of Kilimanjaro will melt in about 20 years' time, so it's best climbed pretty soon!

The other snow-capped East African peak is Mount Kenya, north of the Kenyan capital, Nairobi. This mountain is sacred to the Kikuyu, one of Kenya's many ethnic groups. The two major peaks, Nelion and Batian, are situated at 5,199 metres and 5,189 metres above sea level.

Different types of vegetation can be seen as you climb, from rich alpine forests to bamboo forests, moorlands with giant heather, and finally dry tundra and glaciers at the top. Animal life on the mountain includes giant forest hogs, mongoose and elephants in the lower bamboo forests, and hyrax, duiker and mouse shrews on the higher slopes.

You can hire equipment to climb Mount Kenya in Nairobi, while preparations to climb Mount Kilimanjaro can be made at many tourism and safari operations in Arusha in Tanzania.

Incidentally, Zhao Rugua refers to a "great mountain" west of Zengba, one of the words used to describe East Africa in his 13th century account. Could he have heard of someone who had sighted Mount Kilimanjaro, which lies to the west of Kenya's coast?

**A**n old Zanzibari sits outside his home next to the ornately carved pillars of his door post. Opposite: Mount Kilimanjaro rises majestically from the East African plains in this view from Amboseli National Park in Kenya.

# The End of an Age

On 2 February 1421, the first day of the Lunar New Year, the Yongle emperor presided over the inauguration of his new Ming capital Beijing, the Forbidden City. Thousands of soldiers, officials and foreign envoys gathered to perform the traditional kowtow before the emperor. In the Chinese worldview, his perfect virtue had ensured that all was equally perfect on earth, so all under heaven had gathered to pay tribute to the Son of Heaven.

On the surface everything appeared harmonious. The treasure fleet was bringing back foreign officials happy to be part of China's tribute system. The emperor's treasury had increased enormously and China's knowledge of the world had grown with each new voyage. Cities in Southeast Asia, around the Indian Ocean and in East Africa and Arabia knew the might and power of China and the wisdom of sending tribute to the Middle Kingdom. But was everything as rosy as the colourful spectacle to establish the new city suggested?

To begin with, many of Zhudi's advisors and ministers were against the decision to transfer the capital from Nanjing to Beijing. Quite apart from the fact that they were southerners, they weren't enthusiastic about the sheer cost of building the new capital. Soon after the new capital was inaugurated, records appeared of officials informing the emperor that peasants were starving due to the strains placed on them by the construction of the new capital.[1]

Early morning mist shrouds the huge edifices of the Forbidden City in Beijing (opposite). Above: An outlying building within the Forbidden City complex.

*View of Nanjing painted by an artist who had climbed the famous Porcelain Tower in the city. The tower was built during the Yongle reign with money from voyages of the treasure fleet.*

More drama occurred in the spring after the dedication of the Forbidden City, when during violent storms, lightning struck the three ceremonial halls within the palace enclosure. The magnificent wooden buildings succumbed to flames that raged for more than a day. Zhudi was horrified. Had he offended Heaven? He summoned his advisors and issued an edict that the councillors should point out "if our actions have in fact been improper … lay these out one by one, so that we may try to … regain the favour of Heaven".[2]

Clearly the natural disaster had unsettled Zhudi, for he issued a series of proclamations lifting some of the heavy burdens faced by the peasantry. He returned grain taxes from provinces that had suffered natural disasters and also issued a halt to future voyages of the treasure fleet and banned all preparations for future travel.

Zhudi's empire, however, continued to suffer financial problems, due to the cost of fighting a guerrilla war in Annam and the emperor's expansionist policies concerning the kingdoms of the northern steppe. Less than a year after the disastrous fire at the Forbidden City, Zhudi was on the march west to quell border incursions. Chinese forces did overcome the Uriyangqads, but their leader Arughtai had fled. Both in 1423 and in 1424, the by then aged and sickly Zhudi raised armies to seek out Arughtai but to no avail. On the return journey to Beijing in 1424, overcome by illness, he died on the steppe.

Zhudi's role in the voyages of the treasure fleet cannot be understated. The whole enterprise was driven by his great sense of a renewal of the Chinese universe, and he did all he could to establish the legitimacy and primacy of his new Ming order. From requesting rulers from far-flung lands across vast oceans to come and pay

tribute before the Dragon Throne to constructing the largest surviving medieval palace in the world, from conquering Annam in Vietnam to pacifying the Mongol and Turkic tribes on China's borders, the Yongle emperor was ever mindful of the Mandate of Heaven and his responsibilities as emperor.

Zhudi was succeeded by his son Zhu Gaozhi, whose first edict in 1424 was to cut all unnecessary fiscal expenditure. All voyages of the treasure ships were to be stopped and all ships moored at the mouth of the Yangzi River sent back to Nanjing, their goods confiscated by the Department of Internal Affairs. Foreign envoys returning home would be provided with only a small escort, and officials abroad were ordered back home at once. Also ordered back to their homes were people who had been called upon to take part in future voyages.

The message was crystal clear: China's future lay not at sea, but on land; her wealth and prosperity was not tied to the ocean, trade and commerce but to farmland, agriculture and harvests; and her defence and protection lay with the Great Wall in the north and not an enormous armada of huge, well-armed, nine-masted ships.

The abrupt reversal of the policies of the previous regime was all set to take place when Zhu Gaozhi died in 1425, barely nine months after he ascended the throne. His son Zhu Zhanji, who succeeded him, revived the tribute system, and his reign saw the seventh and last voyage of the treasure fleet. It was to be the largest voyage, with more than 300 ships and 27,500 men.[3]

Before the ships left Chinese shores in January 1432, Zheng He erected a tablet in Changle on the Fujian coast. In it, he documented the achievements of the voyages of the treasure fleet "in unifying

seas and continents". As a result of the journeys, "the countries beyond the horizon from the ends of the earth have all become subjects... bearing precious objects and presents" to the Ming court. The tablet goes on to state the growth in Chinese geographical and scientific knowledge gained by the voyages, how "the distances and routes" between these distant lands "may be calculated". Zheng He added that Chinese culture had also spread far and wide to "manifest the transforming power of imperial virtue."

This voyage was Zheng He's last, for he died at sea on the return voyage. His body was wrapped in white cloth and Islamic prayers were chanted before the corpse was lowered into the ocean. A tombstone was erected in Nanjing, outside the city, where to this day people come to honour his memory.[4]

With the loss of Zheng He in 1433 and the death of Zhu Zhanji in 1435, the steam went out of the expeditions. The new emperor discouraged shipbuilding. Corruption set in, with local officials stealing tribute meant for the emperor. The government gradually lost its monopoly on foreign trade, as goods began to enter China through piracy and smuggling. Piracy also compromised coastal security.

Perhaps a major reason for the end of the treasure ships was the infighting at the imperial court, with eunuchs supporting trade and travel on the one hand, and Confucian advisors supporting traditional agriculture. Court officials issued regulations limiting the size of ships and crew. Eventually, the Longjiang shipyards were closed and the building of all oceangoing ships was prohibited. By 1500, the death penalty was handed down to anyone found guilty of building a boat with more than two masts. Twenty-five years later, an edict from the emperor ordered the destruction of all oceangoing ships and the arrest of merchants found using these ships.

The final nail in the coffin of seagoing enterprises was the Mongol threat from the north. In 1644 the Ming dynasty fell to the Manchus, a Jurchen tribe from the northeast.[5]

What of all the information that the treasure fleet collected on its seven epic voyages? A story goes that in 1477 a eunuch wished to consult the ship logs kept in the archives. The vice president of the Ministry of War, Liu Daxia, got wind of his intent and had them removed. Liu reported to his minister that the logs had been "lost" and added his own take on the voyages:

*The expeditions of San Bao to the West Ocean wasted tens of myriads of money and grain and moreover the people who met their deaths may be counted in the myriads. Although he returned with wonderful, precious things, what benefit was it to the state? This was merely an action of bad government of which ministers should severely disapprove. Even if the old archives were still preserved they should be destroyed in order to suppress (a repetition of these things) at root.*[6]

The Ming navy shrank from 3,500 vessels in the early 15th century to being practically nonexistent a hundred years later. More than that, China lost much knowledge of shipbuilding and related technologies. European powers would slowly find themselves sailing around the world and "discovering" new places. Perhaps it isn't strange then that it is names like Batholomeu Dias, Vasco da Gama, Ferdinand Magellan and Christopher Columbus that we associate today with voyages of exploration and discovery, and not Zheng He's.

**N**ineteenth century print of the harbour at Guangzhou, filled with European trading ships eager to exploit newly-won trade concessions from a weak Qing dynasty.

VUE DE QUANG-CHEU-FU OU CANTON.

# Epilogue

In the *Ming shi* or *History of the Ming Dynasty*, one name among the long list of places that Zheng He visited is Longyamen, literally Dragon's Teeth Gate. Historians have identified it as the Singapore Strait, with some believing it is the island of Singapore, more specifically Keppel Harbour in the southwestern coastal region of modern Singapore.

Singapore was founded in 1819 and became a busy port city almost at once, mainly because no taxes were levied on any trade that took place in the port. The founding father of Singapore, Stamford Raffles, declared that "no sinister, no sordid view, no considerations either of political importance or pecuniary advantage should interfere with the broad and liberal principles on which the British interest have been established (in Singapore)", that "monopoly and exclusive privileges … are here unknown" and that "Singapore will long and always remain a free port and no taxes on trade or industry will be established to check its future rise and prosperity."[1]

This policy of tax-free trade attracted traders from all over Southeast Asia and beyond. Singapore became in the 19th century what Melaka was in the early part of the 15th century during the time of Zheng He's voyages – a vast emporium visited by hundreds of Arab dhows, Bugis schooners, Chinese junks and European vessels. Like Zheng He's ships, these vessels would also depend on monsoon-bearing winds to travel to and from Singapore. So Chinese, Siamese and Vietnamese ships would arrive with the northeast monsoon and return with the southwest monsoon, while Bugis ships would arrive before.

Private shipping enterprises rapidly developed, with some 43 merchant shipping houses established by 1846. Their national origins reflected the cosmopolitan nature of Singapore. British, Jewish, Chinese, Arab, Armenian, German, Portuguese, American and Parsi companies jostled with each other to make as much profit as they possibly could from the trading opportunities that Singapore offered.[2]

The country's trade grew as a result of European capital and Asian, particularly Chinese, enterprise.

The multiracial nature of commercial activity in Singapore was in fact not limited to the19th century. There is some record of a multiethnic trading post on Singapore in *Daoyi Zhilue*, written in 1349 by Wang Dayuan, a trader from Nanzhang in Jianxi. His record of travel in the Nanyang or Southern Ocean lists some 99 places, of which Dan-ma-xie (Temasek, Singapore's Malay name) is one. He recounts trading and events in two areas of Dan-ma-xie – Longyamen and Ban-zu – and notes that in the former area "the natives and the Chinese dwell side by side".

Historians have noted that this is significant because this is the only port in Wang Dayuan's account to mention an overseas Chinese community – and that, too, one living in the midst of indigenous people.[3]

In the 21st century, Singapore continues to rely heavily on shipping and commerce, as it has since ancient times. And the very position of the island, on the trading routes between the Indian Ocean and the South China Sea, has encouraged a bustling, open and multicultural city.

A display of artefacts including a Chinese ship model (opposite) on board a Chinese junk, the venue of the Singapore Tourism Board's media launch of its Zheng He 600th anniversary celebrations.

# Six Hundred Years On...

Six hundred years later, the world is looking again at a China that is opening up once more. The 21st century is being called the Pacific Century, one in which China and the Asia-Pacific region will play a dominant role in world politics, trade and culture. It is fitting then that there are groups and individuals who remember the legacy of Zheng He's voyages and seek to commemorate this remarkable period in Chinese history.

## INTERNATIONAL ZHENG HE SOCIETY
### http://www.chengho.org/

The International Zheng He Society is one of many associations dedicated to the study and appreciation of the early Ming voyages. This particular group of history enthusiasts, both amateur and professional, is based in Singapore. One of its projects marking the 600th anniversary of the voyages involves publishing books on Zheng He in both Chinese and English. Another is the Cheng Ho Cultural Museum in Melaka to showcase the history of the voyages. The society is helping to organise an international Zheng He Exhibition at the new National Library in Singapore. This exhibition showcases contributions of the voyages to maritime history, world culture and science and technology through the use of artefacts and historical documents.

## FRIENDS OF ADMIRAL ZHENG HE
### http://www.admiralzhenghe.org

The Friends of Admiral Zheng He, also based in Singapore, is a group that promotes awareness of the life and achievements of Admiral Zheng He. It is a forum for the exchange of information about Zheng He and his voyages. The group also serves as a community to disseminate research findings and a repository of reference material on Zheng He studies. In this they are aided by the Zheng He Museum, which they established as a focal point for activities related to the voyages of the treasure fleet.

## GAVIN MENZIES AND 1421
### http://www.1421.tv

In 2002, author Gavin Menzies set tongues wagging when he published his book *1421: The Year China Discovered the World*. In it he makes the claim that Zheng He's fleet had circumnavigated the world way before the likes of Dias, Magellan and Columbus. And that the Chinese voyagers subsequently made maps that fell into the hands of the early European explorers. His contention is that the Chinese sailed to the New World before Columbus. He uses many different types of evidence to support his claims. It is possibly because of the controversial nature of his views that there has been so much interest generated in the voyages of the treasure fleet. His book has certainly introduced Zheng He to a new global audience, with *1421* making it to the *New York Times* best-seller list.

## HUAYINET
### http://www.huayinet.org

HuayiNet is a databank on overseas Chinese that was set up in 1998 through the participation of 13 Singapore-based libraries and research, heritage, community and other institutions. Creators of the HuayiNet database, the Inter-Agency Committee on the Chinese Overseas Databank & Research, Singapore, aim to promote wider international access to, and exchange of, information on the Chinese overseas. HuayiNet is also designed as a resource portal for scholars, researchers and others interested in activities of the Chinese overseas. The Inter-Agency Committee, the association of Ohio University Libraries, USA, the International Zhenghe Society, Singapore, and the Friends of Admiral Zheng He, Singapore, are the collective impetus behind the Third International Conference of Institutes and Libraries for Chinese Overseas Studies. The theme of this conference in August 2005, in Singapore, is "Maritime Asia and the Chinese Overseas (1405–2005)".

## NATIONAL LIBRARY BOARD, SINGAPORE, AND THE ZHENG HE AND MARITIME ASIA EXHIBITION
### http://www.visitsingapore-zhenghe.com/ exhibition/index.php

The National Library in Singapore has organised an exhibition on Zheng He and Maritime Asia running from August 2005 to January 2006. The exhibition covers maritime trade from the Tang dynasty up to the beginning of the Republic, a period of more than one thousand years. The focus of this exhibition is on trade, culture, foreign relations, maritime technology and the impact of voyages between the trading countries of maritime Asia. Ancient texts, maps, charts, stone inscriptions, photographs, videos, ship models, sculptures, calligraphy, paintings, and navigational instruments and tools bring this interactive exhibition to life.

## LIBRARY OF CONGRESS
http://www.loc.gov/today/pr/2005/05-105.html

The U.S. Library of Congress in Washington, D.C. hosted a one-day symposium in May 2005. Zheng He scholars gathered there included an oceanographer and hydraulic engineer, a retired British Royal Navy captain, historians, scholars of the Ming dynasty and other researchers. The event was organised by the U.S. Zheng He's Voyages Celebration Council, the Greater Mid-Atlantic Chapter of the Chinese American Librarians Association, the Asian Division Friends Society and the International Publishing House for China's Culture.

The Library has an annotated bibliography of books about Zheng He and his voyages. It gives information on books in different languages and from different periods along with a brief summary for each entry. A useful start for anyone wishing to delve deeper into the world of Zheng He. The online version of the bibliography is at **http://www.chinesedc.com/Zhenghe/research/ZhengHeBibliography.htm**

## SINGAPORE TOURISM BOARD
http://www.visitsingapore-zhenghe.com/

The Singapore Tourism Board is commemorating the 600th anniversary of Zheng He's voyages in a big way. A Zheng He Festive Village at the Marina Promenade at the city's waterfront comprises beautiful pavilions that recreate the ports Zheng He sailed to and give visitors a glimpse of what these places were like during his time. The 1421 Exhibition is a blockbuster showcase of Gavin Menzies' bestseller *1421: The Year China Discovered the World*. Then there is a new musical production, *The Admiral's Odyssey*, by Action Theatre at Jubilee Hall and a symbolic recreation of Longyamen at Labrador Park. The STB has been involved in coordinating the Zheng He festivities in Singapore, including the Zheng He and Maritime Asia Exhibition at the National Library and the Third International Conference of Institutes and Libraries for Chinese Overseas at the Regional Language Centre.

## SYMPOSIUM IN MEMORY OF THE 600TH ANNIVERSARY OF ZHENG HE'S FIRST EXPEDITION
http://www.jsass.com.cn/article_show.asp?ArticleID=358

The Central Committee of the Chinese Communist Party and the People's Government of Jiangsu Province is hosting a seminar in Nanjing and Taicang in July 2005 on the theme

"Open to the World, Peace and Development" to celebrate the 600th anniversary of Zheng He's expeditions. Jiangsu province, where Zheng He spent a major part of his life, is the site of many well-preserved Zheng He-related artefacts.

## CELEBRATIONS IN CHINA
http://www.moc.gov.cn/zhenghe600/default.htm

This Chinese website gives a comprehensive list of events commemorating the 600th anniversary of Zheng He's voyages.

## ZHENG HE TRAIL
http://www.zhenghetrail.com/

Zheng He enthusiasts can walk in the footsteps of the admiral with a specially designed tour. The Zheng He Trail takes travellers to Zheng He sites and temples in Singapore and Malaysia on a voyage of discovery that blends history with holiday. Participants can soak in the cultural diversity of Malaysia and Singapore while exploring the legends surrounding the great seafarer.

## ROUND-THE-WORLD RESEARCH CRUISE

The China Ocean Mineral Resources Research and Development Association has organised a 300-day oceanic voyage around the world. On board, scientists and researchers will conduct a host of scientific experiments. The research voyage is part of the 600th anniversary celebrations of Zheng He's voyages.

# Notes

## 1. The Middle Kingdom

1 Perkins, Dorothy, *Encyclopedia of China – The Essential Reference to China, Its History and Culture*, London, 1999.

2 Zheng Hesheng and Zheng Yijun, *Zheng He xia Xiyang ziliao huibian* (*Collections of research materials on Zheng He's voyage to the Western Oceans*), Jinan, 1980–89, II:2, p. 1152, quoting Xia Xie, *Ming tong jian* (*Comprehensive mirror of Ming history*) [1873], Beijing, 1959, chapter 14; Levathes, Louise, *When China Ruled the Seas*, New York, 1994, p. 73.

3 Perkins, Dorothy, op. cit.

4 Anonymous, *Shun feng xiang song* (*Fair winds for escort*) [c. 1430], in Xiang Da, *Liang zhong hai dao zhen jing* (*Two classics on navigation by compass*), Beijing, 1961, pp. 23–24.

5 Hook, Brian, and Twitchett, Dennis C., editors, *Cambridge Encyclopedia of China*, Cambridge, 1991.

## 2. Zheng He and China's Islamic Tradition

1 Zhou Zhongyu, editor, *Zheng He jiapu kaoshi* (*Investigation into the family history of Zheng He*, a compilation of texts inscribed on tablets that relate to Zheng He and his family), Kunming, 1937, p. 10; Levathes, op. cit., p. 64.

2 Dillon, Michael, *China's Muslims*, Oxford, 1996.

3 Zhou Zhongyu, op. cit.

4 Tsai, Henry, *Perpetual Happiness – The Ming Emperor Yongle*, Seattle, 2002, p. 38; F.W. Mote, *Imperial China 900–1800*, Cambridge, 2003, p. 614.

5 *Quanzhou Yisilanjiao shike* (*Islamic inscriptions in Quanzhou [Zaiton]*), Chen Dasheng, compiler, Quanzhou, 1984, p. 11; Levathes, op. cit., p. 147.

6 Booz, Patrick, R., *Yunnan*, Hong Kong, 1997.

7 Zhou Zhongyu, op. cit., pp. 1–2.

8 Bonavia, Judy, *The Silk Road*, Hong Kong, 2002.

9 Neville-Hadley, Peter, *China and the Silk Routes*, London, 1997.

10 Hollege, Simon, *Xi'an, China's Ancient Capital*, Hong Kong, 2000.

## 3. The Journeys Begin

1 *Song shi* (*Official history of the Song dynasty*) c. 1345, 186: 9-9; Wu Qian, *Xu Guo gong zou yi* (*Memorials submitted to the throne by the duke of Xu Guo*) [1231–60], in *Shi wan zhuan lou congshu* (*Collectanea of the hall of one hundred thousand volumes*), published 1876–92, 3:5; Levathes, op. cit., p. 43.

2 Lo Jung-pang, "China's paddle-wheel boats; the mechanical craft used in the opium war and their historical background", *Qinghua Journal of Chinese Studies*, Taiwan, 5, 1958, pp. 189–211; Levathes, op. cit., pp. 46–47.

3 Levathes, op. cit., pp. 50–53.

4 Needham, Joseph, *Science and Civilisation in China*, Cambridge, England, 1971, IV: 2, section 27, Cambridge, 1965; Levathes, op. cit., p. 45.

5 *Taizong shi lu*, chapters 19, 21, 23, 26, 35, 38, 39, 46, 52 and 54, in *Ming shi lu* (*Veritable records of the Ming dynasty*) [1368–1644], Taipei, 1962–64; Xi Longfei and He Guowei, "Shilun Zheng He baochuan de chuanxing yu jianzao didian" (A preliminary discussion of the ship type of Zheng He's treasure ship and places where the ships were built), in *Zheng He yu Fujian* (*Zheng He and Fujian*), Fujian, 1986, p. 106; Levathes, op. cit., p. 75.

6 Menzies, Gavin, *1421: The Year China Discovered the World*, London, 2002, pp. 51–52.

7 Levathes, op. cit., p. 75.

8 Keith, Donald H. and Buys, Christian J., "New light on medieval Chinese seagoing ship construction", *International Journal of Nautical Archaeology and Underwater Exploration*, 10: 2, 1981, pp. 119–32; Levathes, op. cit., p. 81.

9 Chen Yenhang et al., "Zheng He bao chuan fuyuan yanjiu" (Research on the reconstruction of Zheng He's treasure ship), *Chuan shi yanjiu* (*Studies of shipbuilding history*), 2, 1986; Levathes, op. cit., p. 80.

10 Levathes, op. cit., p. 80.

11 Levathes, op. cit., pp. 81–82.

12 Luo Maodong, *San Bao taijian Xiyang ji tongsu yan yi* (*Journey of the three-jewelled eunuch to the Western Oceans*) [1597], Shanghai, 1985.

13 Luo, op. cit., chapter 15; Zheng Hesheng, *Zheng He*, Sichuan, 1945, I, pp. 204–206; Levathes, op. cit., pp. 82–83.

14 Zheng Hesheng, op. cit., pp. 144–150; Ma Huan, *Ying yai sheng lan* (*The Overall Survey of the Ocean Shores*) [1451], translated by J.V.G. Mills, Hakluyt Series, Cambridge, 1970, pp. 31–32; Levathes, op. cit., p. 83.

## 4. To Melaka, Indonesia and Longyamen

1 Marks, Robert B., *Tigers, Rice, Silk & Silt. Environment and Economy in Late Imperial South China*, Cambridge, 1998; Cushman, Jennifer, *Fields from the Sea: Chinese Junk Trade with Siam during the late Eighteenth and Early Nineteenth centuries*, Ithaca, 1993.

2 Hanum, Zakiah, *Historical Origins of Malaysian States*, Selangor, 2004, p. 41.

3 *Taizong shi lu*, op. cit., chapter 47; Levathes, op. cit., p. 108.

4 *Taizong shi lu*, op. cit., chapter 47.

5 Ma Huan, op. cit., pp. 113–14.

6 Ma Huan, op. cit., p. 84.

7 Ma Huan, op. cit., p. 113.

8 *Insight Guides Malaysia*, APA Publications, 1998.

9 Wolters, O.W., *The Fall of Sri Vijaya in Malay History*, London, 1970, pp. 49–76; Levathes, op. cit., pp. 98–99.

10 Zheng Hesheng and Zheng Yijun, op. cit., pp. 1563–67, citing *Taizong shi lu*, chapters 51, 71; Levathes, op. cit., p. 102.

11 Zheng Hesheng, op. cit., II:2, p. 1593, citing Xia Xie, op. cit., chapter 16; Levathes, op. cit., pp. 139, 142.

12 Ma Huan, op. cit., pp. 93, 94, 97; Levathes, op. cit., pp. 99–100.

13 Miksic, John N., "14th century Singapore: a port of trade", in *Early Singapore 1300s–1819*, editors John N. Miksic and Cheryl-Ann Low Mei Gek, Singapore, 2004, pp. 41–54.

## 5. To Sri Lanka and India's Spice Coast

1 Ma Huan, op. cit., pp. 127–28; quoted in Levathes, op. cit., p. 100.

2 Needham, Joseph, op. cit., IV:3, section 29, "Nautics", pp. 552–53; Levathes, op. cit., p. 113.

3 Perera, Edward, "Alakeswara: His Life and Times", *Journal of the Malayan Branch of the Royal Asiatic Society*, 18:55 (1904), p. 291; Levathes, op. cit., pp. 114–18.

4 Zheng Hesheng, op. cit., II:2, p. 1577, quoting *Ming shi lu*, 1368–1644; *Taizong shi lu*, op. cit., chapter 77; Levathes, op. cit., p. 115.

5 Yang Rong, *Yang Wenmin gong ji* (*Collected works of Yang Rong*), Jianan, 1515, chapter 1; Levathes, op. cit., p. 115.

6 Perera, op. cit., pp. 291–95; Levathes, op. cit., p. 116.

7 *Ming bei ben ta Tang Xiyu ji* (*Ming edition of the Record of the Western Regions in the Tang*) [1440], taken from Sun Zongwen, "Zheng He xia Xiyang hongfa shiji" (Achievements in spreading Buddhist doctrines during Zheng He's voyages), *Zheng He Yanjiu* (*Zheng He Studies*), 13, November 1991, pp. 58–59; Levathes, op. cit., p. 117.

8 Perera, Edward, "The Age of Sri Pakakama Bahu IV", *Journal of the Ceylon Branch of the Royal Asiatic Society*, 22:63, 1910, p. 17; Levathes, op. cit., p. 117.

9 Needham, op. cit.; Levathes, op. cit., p. 113.

10 Aves, Edward, *Footprint Sri Lanka*, Bath, 2003.

11 Ma Huan, op. cit., p. 138; Levathes, op. cit., p. 106.

12 Levathes, op. cit., p. 100.

13 Ma Huan, op. cit., p. 140; Levathes, op. cit., p. 100.

14 Ma Huan, op. cit., p. 141; Levathes, op. cit., p. 101.

15 Ma Huan, op. cit., p. 141.

16 Ma Huan, op. cit., p. 139; Levathes, op. cit., p. 101.

17 Xia Xie, op. cit., pp. 874–75.

18 *Taizong shi lu*, op. cit., chapter 183; Levathes, op. cit., pp.145, 223–24

19 *Lonely Planet Kerala*, Australia, 2000.

**6. To the Persian Gulf and Arabia Felix**

1 Levathes, op. cit., p. 137.

2 Quoted at the 1416 dedication of the Jinghai Temple in Nanjing; translated by Levathes, op. cit., p. 137.

3 Levathes, op. cit., pp. 138, 140.

4 Ma Huan, op. cit., pp. 165–72; Levathes, op. cit., p. 140.

5 *Insight Guides Yemen*, APA Publications, 1997.

6 Stark, Freya, *The Coasts of Incense*, London, 1953.

7 Ma Huan, op. cit., p. 155; Levathes, op. cit., p. 149.

8 Chaudhuri, K.N., "A note on Ibn Taghri Birdi's description of Chinese ships in Aden and Jedda", *Journal of the Royal Asiatic Society of Great Britain and Ireland*, 1, 1989, p. 112; Levathes, op. cit., p. 171.

9 Levathes, op. cit., p. 171.

**7. To Africa's Swahili Coast**

1 Duyvendak, J.J.L., "The true dates of the Chinese maritime expeditions in the early fifteenth century," *T'oung Pao 32*, 1939, pp. 382–83, translation of a poem by Jin Youzi in Yan Congjian, *Shu yu zhou zi lu*, chapter 9; Levathes, op. cit., p. 151.

2 Levathes, op. cit., pp. 140–42.

3 Duyvendak, op. cit., p. 404, quoting a poem by Shen Du, who was commissioned to paint the giraffe; Levathes, op. cit., pp. 141–42.

4 Duyvendak, op. cit., p. 405, citing *Ming shi* (*Official history of the Ming dynasty*) [1739], editors, Zhang Tingyu et al., Beijing, 1974, chapter 326; Levathes, op. cit., p. 143.

5 Levathes, op. cit., pp. 142–43, 172–73.

6 "The Giraffe and Sino-African Friendship", article by Lin Minyang in *People's Daily*, Beijing, 16 January 1983; Snow, Philip, *The Star Raft: China's Encounter with Africa*, New York, 1988, p. 1.

7 Duyvendak, J.J.L., "China's Discovery of Africa", London, *Probsthain*, Lectures given at London University, 1947, p. 22; translation of Zhou Qufei, *Ling wai da dai* (*[Written] in place of replies about [the southwestern regions] beyond the mountain passes*) [1178]; Levathes, op. cit., p. 37.

8 Snow, op. cit., p. 13.

9 Freeman-Grenville, G.S.P., *The East African Coast: Select Documents from the First to the Earlier Nineteenth Century*, London, 1975, p. 8; translation of Duan Chengshi, *Yuyang za zu* (*Miscellany of Yuyang Mountain*) [863]; Levathes, op. cit., p. 37.

10 Duyvendak, J.J.L., "China's Discovery of Africa" London, op. cit., p. 24; translation of Zhu Yu, *Pingzhou ke tan* (*From chats in Pingzhou*) [1119]; Levathes, op. cit., p. 38.

11 Snow, op. cit., p. 12.

12 Hirth, Friedrich and Roderick, W.W., *Chau Ju-kua: His Work on the Chinese and Arab Trade in the 12th and 13th centuries*, St Petersburg, 1911; Snow, op. cit., pp. 13–14.

13 Hirth, Friedrich and Roderick, W.W., op. cit.; Snow, op. cit., pp. 13–14.

14 Snow, op. cit., p. 14.

15 Fei Xin, *Xing cha sheng lan* (*Marvellous visions from the star raft*) [1436], Shanghai, 1938. Partial translation in Gabriele Foccardi, *The Chinese travelers of the Ming period*, Wiesbaden, 1986, pp. 71, 73. Levathes, op. cit., p. 151.

16 Duyvendak, J.J.L., "Desultory notes on the *Hsi Yang Chi*" ([Luo Maodeng's novel of 1597 based on the voyages of Zheng He], *T'oung Pao 42*, 1953, p. 18.

17 Gong Zhen, *Xiyang fan guo zhi* (*Record of foreign countries in the Western Oceans*) [1434], Beijing, 1961.

18 Snow, op. cit., p. 5, quoted in Wheatley, Paul, "Analecta Sino-Africana Recensa", in *East Africa and the Orient; Cultural Syntheses in Pre-Colonial times*, ed. Neville Chittick and R.I. Rotberg, Nairobi, 1975.

19 Snow, op. cit., pp. 5–6.

20 Levathes, op. cit., pp. 198-203.

21 Freeman-Grenville, op. cit., p. 143; Levathes, op. cit., p. 198.

**8. The End of an Age**

1 Goodrich and Fang, editors, *Dictionary of Ming Biography*, p. 360; quoted in Tsai, Henry, op. cit., p. 127.

2 Shang Chuan, *Yongle huang di* (*The Yongle Emperor*), Beijing, 1989, pp. 214–15, quoting *Taizong shi lu*, op. cit., chapter 149; Levathes, op. cit., p. 158.

3 Levathes, op. cit., p. 169.

4 Changle tablet of 1431, translated by Duyvendak, in "The true dates of the Chinese maritime expeditions in the early fifteenth century", op. cit.; Levathes, op. cit., p. 170.

5 Levathes, op. cit., pp. 173–81.

6 Duyvendak, pp. 395–598, from Gu Qiyuan, *Ke zuo zhiu yu* (*Idle talks with guests*), p. 1; Su Wangxiang, "Zheng He Xi yang dang'an wei Liu Daxia shaohui shu zhiyi" (Doubts about the reporting of Zheng He's logs being burned by Liu Daxia), *Zheng He Yanjiu* (*Zheng He Studies*), November 1990, pp. 11, 39–43; Levathes, op. cit., pp. 179–80.

**Epilogue**

1 Turnbull, C.M., *A History of Singapore, 1918–1988*, Oxford, 1989, p. 22.

2 Turnbull, op. cit., p. 39.

3 Miksic, John, op. cit., pp. 43–45.

# Picture Credits